WHEN ROCK
WAS YOUNG

OTHER BOOKS BY BRUCE POLLOCK

1975   In Their Own Words: Pop Songwriting, 1955–1974
1977   Playing for Change (Novel)
1978   Me, Minsky & Max (Novel)
1978   The Face of Rock & Roll (with John Wagman)
1979   The Disco Handbook
1980   It's Only Rock and Roll (Novel)
1980   The Rock 'n' Roll Fun Book

HOLT, RINEHART AND WINSTON • NEW YORK

When *ROCK* Was *Young*

A NOSTALGIC REVIEW OF
THE *Top 40* ERA

BRUCE POLLOCK

Acknowledgments

Thanks to Marcia Vance and Frank Zaino.

Copyright © 1981 by Bruce Pollock
All rights reserved, including the right to reproduce
this book or portions thereof in any form.
Published by Holt, Rinehart and Winston,
383 Madison Avenue, New York, New York 10017.
Published simultaneously in Canada by Holt, Rinehart
and Winston of Canada, Limited.

■

Library of Congress Cataloging in Publication Data
Pollock, Bruce.
When rock was young.
Discography: p.
Includes index.
1. Rock music—United States—History and criticism.
2. Music, Popular (Songs, etc.)—United States—
History and criticism. 3. Rock musicians—United
States—Biography. I. Title
ML3534.P64   784.5'4'00973   80-23460
ISBN Hardcover: 0-03-049836-8
ISBN Paperback: 0-03-049841-4

■

First Edition
Designer: Amy Hill
Printed in the United States of America
1 3 5 7 9 10 8 6 4 2

For Walter Wager: I owed you one.

Contents

PART TWO: SINGERS

Four pages of photographs follow page 119.

WHEN ROCK WAS YOUNG

Introduction

*I*n 1955 or thereabouts a new sound invaded the record charts of America. Propounded by a frantic core of dedicated disc jockeys, emanating from certain plucky, almost mythical radio stations buried far beneath the pop-spewing giants, this new sound came to be known as rock 'n' roll. It was a beat that became a language that became a culture.

Call it rhythm and blues, country and western, or rockabilly, as a beat it was undeniably big, raw, rough, uncivilized, and unpredictable. As a language it spoke more directly and with more force to a teenage generation than any vocalist, big band, or dance marathon. Its raucous sweep encompassed fads, fashions, slang, bodily posture, and movements. Instantly understood and easily digested by its impressionable audience, the language imparted by the sound fostered a sense of identity, of union, of an unbroken whole—young America wired together by wireless—that was capable of causing great changes, or at least a little havoc.

It would be years before discerning commentators would begin applying the word *culture* to the rock 'n' roll audience, perhaps because most commentators assumed it didn't have any. The sound it championed was regarded by most adults as kid stuff at best, a passing concoction as droolingly effervescent as a cherry Coke, and just as gassy. At worst, it was seen

1

as something more intoxicating and insidious (which, of course, it was), a veritable plot against the motherland, complete with amoral instructions delivered by barbaric delinquents, themselves no more than puppets manipulated by the unseen dirty hands of nameless exploiters. (This also turned out to be a fairly accurate appraisal, although it took quite a while before most teenagers realized it.)

The 1955 movie *Blackboard Jungle* had given the generation a powerful myth. When Elvis Presley swaggered so despicably onto "The Ed Sullivan Show" that he had to be censored below the waist, the myth expanded, proliferating in towns and villages where it was taken up by otherwise harmless youths affecting ducktails and leather jackets, garrison belts and white socks. But aside from an occasional riot at a rock 'n' roll show, the barbarism was more latent than actual. In fact, the TV-boom war babies who would suffer their adolescence attuned to the chord changes of rock 'n' roll from 1955 to 1963—the generation that preceded Woodstock, FM radio, the album-buying market, and the coming of the Beatles—were essentially a passive bunch, listeners who preferred to contemplate the fantasy world handed them on a 45 RPM wax platter by a succession of faceless singers and groups. They listened to wild-sounding boys and angel-voiced girls (and vice versa), most of them raving innocents out for glory and love who would soon disappear into an anonymous landscape only to be replaced by others in the endless hit parade.

Apart from what might be construed as an incipient statement of maverick political style, the predilections of the rock 'n' roll crowd figured little in the larger societal picture. The late fifties were a relatively tranquil time in which the prevailing political currents swirled far above the head of the typical kid on the street. And conversely, unlike today, rock 'n' roll was considered beneath media attention. There were no newspaper sections devoted to its fiery gossip; there was no rock press, with its resident critics and philosophers to offer astute assessments. There were only the fan magazines, incessantly extolling the Disneyland antics of Annette Funicello and her assortment of mouse-eared followers. Pat's white shoes, Elvis's induction, and Ricky Nelson's pet peeves were the pristine stuff of these pulpy pages. The occasional paternity suit, the odd drug addict, or the fallen woman was never heard about, never exposed. Only when an unfortunate rocker went down in flames in a plane or car was the fantasy world breached for a day or so.

Otherwise it was business as usual on the Top 40. Ah, Top 40. For statistics freaks, sociologists, and buffs of various denominations, the Top 40 charts—taken from the pages of trade magazines like *Cashbox* and *Billboard*, or offered by those individual favorite radio stations—were from 1955 to 1963 (and to some extent are again today) the Great Steeplechase of Pop, a universal standard of minimal success adhered to by the music industry come Elvis, come payola, come Beatles; a standard as solemn and enduring and unquestioned as TV's Nielsens. Songs outside the pale of the Top 40 rarely got radio play, while songs within those magic precincts were played *ad nauseam*. But what made one song crest at Number 41, another glide to Number 7? Was it in the grooves, the stars, or simply a matter of industry double-dealing? Who knew for sure? Defying analysis, the nimble and unforgiving logic of the Top 40 system controlled not only all the songs the populace got to hear, how many times and even in what order, but the very careers of the voices printed alongside the titles.

And yet, what a heritage of song it has given us. What wonderful, mad singles: three minutes of heaven recorded in basements and garages, bathrooms (for echo) and ramshackle studios, and released via shoestring labels from Clovis, New Mexico, to New Haven, Connecticut. What a collected literature of teenage arcana. Within it lurk all hints of politics, all history—a self-contained vision of the world. It may have been a fantasy vision, but even a cursory study of the Top 40 music of that era reveals that, at least sociologically, it was not blind. A big early phenomenon was racial mix, with black singers and groups enjoying unprecedented popularity with an integrated audience, gaining precious Top 40 ground each year; then Motown Records, presided over by Berry Gordy, came along to solidify those gains. Woman's place on the charts, at least in song, if not in the industry itself, was hotly contested, with a wild and bipartisan debate studding the Top 40 for three anguished years.

And every afternoon, through the still magical world of television, the fantasy became flesh on "American Bandstand," hosted by Dick Clark, where a generation got to watch itself grow up, change clothes, sport ponytails, learn to dance.

By 1960 that teenage fantasy world was getting nudged by adult reality. The machinations of the music industry were brought to public scrutiny by a Senate subcommittee, spurred by the TV quiz-show scandals. The assorted payola revelations only served to give notice that rock 'n' roll wasn't, after all, so different from the rest of society. The merchants and mavens of Tin Pan Alley, meanwhile, had adapted their patented pop techniques to the fancies of the rock 'n' roll audience, a fact of commerce that went virtually unnoticed or certainly unremarked on by that audience, at least in my neighborhood. By then Elvis was on his way to Las Vegas, via Hollywood and Germany, Little Richard was looking for a higher meaning, and Jerry Lee Lewis was banned from the airwaves. Buddy Holly, Chuck Willis, and Eddie Cochran were dead. The Everly Brothers were millionaires. Social awareness was still uncynical, however, and if there were thoughts of protest in the first years of the sixties, such thoughts remained well underground.

In 1962 "the twist" was taken up by the young president's young wife, and by other high-minded socialites the world over. The ensuing "cult of youth" gave rock 'n' roll a new visibility, along with a taste of belated glamour; more important, it primed the press for the coming of the Beatles in February 1964. The Beatles were the first rock 'n' rollers to be taken seriously by the adult world. They were also the first media event, as well as the beneficiaries of uncommon good timing. "If they'd tried to come over in November 1963," comments top press agent of the era, Connie DeNave, "they'd have bombed."

In November 1963, the young president went down in front of a rock 'n' roll generation finally old enough to understand the implications and tragedy of that event, unshielded by Top 40 fantasies. The mourning would continue for the rest of the decade. After Dallas, protest music would erupt from Greenwich Village and travel cross-country to San Francisco, lining up passengers at every local stop along the way. A great percentage of the rock 'n' roll audience would continue to be wired by wireless through the sixties, forming an "alternate culture," eventually an "alternate wavelength"—FM radio— which featured the soundtrack of their coming of age in a language unknown to the Top 40. Suddenly, the Top 40 was revealed as the establishment opinion it had become.

The alternate culture, or wavelength, gave birth to the alternate press, one of whose functions was to chart rock music in depth, all its passionate minutiae, with personalities given faces, warts and all, to go with their famous names. Ultimately, rock 'n' roll during the post-Kennedy depression, through the reign of the Beatles, would become too serious, too preoccupied and self-righteous. It would celebrate its own munificence in complex seventeen-minute odes sung to the twang of a sitar. The three-minute single became subsumed by the longplaying album, and those pioneering, AM radio disc jockeys were regarded with scorn by their slow-talking FM counterparts. The original faceless rock 'n' rollers were put down by the new *artistes* of Rock.

Scoffed at by critics, ignored by cognoscenti and commoners alike, challenged finally in its once exclusive bastion by the FM car stereo, the Top 40 languished. AM radio became an aural boob tube, home of such irrelevant entities as the Archies, the Osmonds, and the Partridge Family, its development arrested at puberty.

However, with the onset of the seventies, and the "alternate culture" laid to rest at Woodstock, at Altamont, on the streets of Chicago, and on the playing fields of Kent State—taking the "alternate wavelength" down with it, along with most of the "alternate press"—rock 'n' roll floundered for the longest time, needing the dire threat of disco music to turn it, at last, back to its Top 40 forebears. In the late seventies the pendulum started swinging back toward the simpler sort of rock 'n' roll always favored by AM radio, the lean and spontaneous sounds, bursting with energy and fervor, championed by the original heroes so long in disrepute.

This, then, seems like the best of times to have another look at rock 'n' roll's first great era, the years 1955 to 1963. With the rock 'n' roll single making a comeback, as released by a post-Beatles third generation of kids, in some cases on their own scrappy, independent labels, a fond retrospective of Top 40's grandest epoch seems to be eminently called for, its small triumphs pinpointed, its movers and shakers given their due.

As I hope my text will indicate, if not necessarily put into words, the age of innocence has long since passed us by, but our fantasies are still stored alphabetically in a leatherette case, along with our original 45s, and buried deep in the closet. Here, however, while there's still time, are the gladiators and handmaidens who formed those fantasies, who in some sense formed us. They were out there on the front lines even before those lines were drawn, for they *drew* the lines while the rest of us were safe at home listening in on the radio. For most of them rock 'n' roll is still their only means of expression; for the rest it's a distant dreamlike memory. Whatever, back then they sent the rock rolling on its turbulent coast-to-coast ride, now in its fourth decade. Without them we'd have been just another silent generation.

Part ONE : Songs

WOLFMAN JACK (SMITH)

■

Deejay

"Your biggest records in the late fifties were mostly your black artists. Fats Domino, Little Richard, all these black artists were copied by people like Elvis Presley and Jerry Lee Lewis. The original rock 'n' roll sound came from the black people and the white people jumped in and started doing the same thing with a country twang, and we had rockabilly.

"All the best jocks, the ones who were really clever and really doing it and creating big audiences were the be-bop jocks in New York City: Jocko, Dr. Jive, Mr. Blues; Alan Freed at first, called himself Moondog [and had to drop the name when he came to New York, in deference to a popular street singer of the same name]. All these guys started by playing rhythm and blues, black 'race' music; they copped it and called it rock 'n' roll. I was doing the same thing when I started in 1960, on XERS in Del Rio, Texas, a 250,000-watt station that covered North America. If you drove from New York to Los Angeles you couldn't lose the station—1570 on the dial. It was the most powerful commercial radio station in the world at that time.

"Back in those days I was running the radio station, doing everything. I was on from midnight to four, selling mail-order record packages, more weight and less weight pills, and playing rhythm and blues—Jimmy Reed, B. B. King. The preachers were on before that. We didn't have contests; we didn't have phones. There were no ratings services like you have to-day; nobody was counting how many people of what age were listening. But I knew we were doing very well with the mail order items; we used to get in the neighborhood of a thousand letters a day.

"I tried to stay away from promotion men; that's where your extreme hype comes in. I tried to stay mostly by the charts, and played what the world was telling me people wanted to hear. I've been on the airwaves now for twenty years doing basically the same thing. As long as I can remember there've been lists, Top 40 lists in the trade magazines, and in my life since 1960 I've been going by the goddamned charts. You didn't vary too far. There's no disc jockey alive who can make a record happen. All you can do is give it exposure. A record gets promoted in your smaller markets, your medium markets. If it's a hit in a medium market, then a radio station will go on it in Los Angeles or New York. It's the same process that's been working now for the past thirty years, even before we had totally boring program directors like we have now.

"Three-fourths of all the oldies are not being played anymore because the program directors have decided they don't appeal to their particular age group. Rock today is all so computerized; it's so well planned that they're boring us to death. Back in those days we didn't give a shit whether a record crossed over from rhythm and blues to Top 40 or not. It was not the thing that you have going today where it's so important that a country artist cross over because he'll sell a million more albums. The dollar value was not put on as much as it is today. That's why the record companies are hurting, that's why radio is hurting for good entertainment. Because the music is not as good as it used to be. Every artist is doing the same thing, into the same groove. They should take their computers and stick them in the toilet and just go by a gut feeling.

"The only salvation for AM radio is to go back to personality and just do zany, unpredictable things which would make people listen. They can listen to FM radio and get bored to death because they know they're going to hear the top ten records every hour, and they also know they're going to get one from the top twenty every hour, and one from the top thirty, or twenty-five; whatever it's down to now.

"I'm looking for things to clear up a little bit in 1980. We'll get some new artists who've got a new way of doing things. There are a lot of things happening in punk rock, new wave. Eventually people will emerge from that kind of atmosphere. Things can't continue the way they're going now. In the old days you had the opportunity to switch from station to station and hear the songs you wanted. Now they don't want to give you that opportunity anymore."

YEARBOOK 1955

.■

*a*s showcased weekly on TV's "Your Hit Parade," pop music had been humming along ever since the days when the Top 40 was only the top ten. The populace thralled to barbershop baritones and blowsy blonde sopranos burbling of sweet romance, as orchestrated by the several reigning czars of Tin Pan Alley. The songs were lulling and bathetic. But in 1955 pop music went head to head with rhythm and blues, sweat at the armpits, blood on the knees. No sooner would a rhythm and blues outfit release a primal love song than one of pop's entrenched majority would stamp out an emasculated version. With all the power of the status quo behind them, these pop renditions generally followed a red carpet to the top of the charts, while the rougher, more authentic r&b originals were barred at the door.

There was "Earth Angel" released by the Penguins, covered by the Crew-cuts (the Crew-cuts had started the whole thing in 1954 with their remake of "Sh-boom," a song first written and sung by the Chords, to considerably less success). "Sincerely" by the Moonglows, went to the top of the charts as rendered by the McGuire Sisters. Georgia Gibbs topped La-Vern Baker & the Gliders on "Tweedle Dee" (Georgia later put out "Dance with Me, Henry," a bowdlerized version of

11

Hank Ballard's "Work with Me, Annie" and its toned-down successor, "Roll with Me, Henry" by Etta James). No less a rhythm and blues figure than Johnny Ace had to fight Teresa Brewer to a standoff for bragging rights to "Pledging My Love." But the chief perpetrator of this bogus art was undoubtedly Pat (real name, Charles) Boone, who brought Fats Domino's "Ain't That a Shame" to the top of the *Billboard* chart (the Top 40 of record) by mid-1955. In September he was back in the top ten again with "At My Front Door," originally released by the El Dorados. Also hard at work were the Fontane Sisters, who took on the Charms' "Hearts of Stone" (itself an interpretation of a 1954 r&b hit by the Jewels), the Marigolds' "Rollin' Stone," "Daddy-O" by Bonnie Lou, and "Adorable" by the Drifters.

That white singers and groups could consistently make rhythm and blues palatable to the radio masses was a mixed blessing to the black creators of this music. On the one hand, they were earning songwriter royalties (unless, as was often the case, they had sold the copyrights to the publisher); exposure in the mass market meant many more dollars than could be earned in the limited reaches of the r&b underground. But, in most cases, the mass audience was totally unaware of the roots from which the songs it was swooning to had sprung. Pop arrangers and stylists went to great pains and absurd lengths to filter whatever was fresh (or raunchy) out of the r&b originals. Thus tunes like "Sh-boom" and "Hearts of Stone" came to be associated with the singers who made them popular, who would go on to long-running success, while the black creators would end up, more often than not, back at their day jobs. Only the lonely few who listened to the r&b stations in 1954–55, who caught on to Alan Freed at the beginning, knew the truth, but it would be a while before their voices would be strong enough to pierce the static pop scene of the mid-fifties.

Perhaps the only white voice in 1955 capable of delivering this black music to the Top 40 in a reasonably unadulterated form belonged to Bill Haley, a banjo player's son from Highland Park, Michigan. In "Rock Around the Clock," a Number 1 song that year, Haley even named the beast. As sung by Bill and his group, the Comets, in the movie *Blackboard Jungle*, the song became rock 'n' roll's first anthem. But Haley had named the beast before that, in "Rock-a-Beating Boogie," which he wrote in 1952. He named it again in "Mambo Rock," released two months before "Rock Around the Clock." He spelled it out more clearly in March 1956, with "R-O-C-K," followed in July by a cover of Little Richard's "Rip It Up," and in October by "Rudy's Rock," which was effectively his Top 40 swan song. (Although "Skinny Minnie" did hit the top twenty in 1958, Bill was by then back to playing weddings; the Comets had become the Jodimars, with no significant change of luck.)

In 1955 four men of considerable rock 'n' roll/r&b stature invaded the Top 40—two black, two white; a singer, two songwriters, and a singer/songwriter. One of the few rhythm and blues records to make it to the Top 40 without being covered by a white act was "Speedo," by the Cadillacs; its rise was perhaps due to the specific nature of the lyrics, as sung by Earl Carroll, which exclaimed, "People often call me Speedo, but my real name is Mr. Earl." No way Pat Boone could get a handle on that (although Pat did have a hit with a song called "Speedy Gonzales" in 1962). In 1960 Earl Carroll went on to join the Coasters, one of the most popular groups to come out of the rhythm and blues era. Most of the Coasters' material— some of the greatest songs the Top 40 has ever known, like "Searching," "Yakety Yak," "Poison Ivy," and "What About Us"—was written by the white songwriting duo, Jerry Leiber & Mike Stoller, whose first appearance on the Top 40, at Number 6 in fact, occurred in 1955 when their studio demo singers known as the Cheers (including the latter-day TV personality Bert Convy) gave us "Black Denim Trousers and Motorcycle Boots," a deft satire of the same wild ones made popular by *Blackboard Jungle*.

The fourth visitor to the charts, up from underground, was

Chuck Berry, who with songs like "Maybellene," his top-five item that year, succeeded in making the black experience universal. His amalgam of black and white sensibilities, pop and rhythm and blues plus the soul and sweat of countless nameless black musicians, was the foundation upon which the children of rock 'n' roll built a monument.

YEARBOOK 1956

*he first white teenagers to pick up on rhythm and blues, tailoring it for their own nefarious ends, were primarily from the country, the sticks, that vast rural nowhere that existed well beyond the consciousness of the average city kid. Desperate, skinny youths they were, from the South and Southwest, who'd grown up wild and cavity-prone, prowling gas stations and five and dimes for that first Coca-Cola of the morning and listening to the doleful laments of Hank Williams on country stations as obscure and funky as those that played rhythm and blues. So, when Elvis Presley started kicking up some dust on the Memphis–Nashville run, got too big for country music to contain him (actually, his records showed up on the country, rhythm and blues, *and* pop charts; all things to all people), and his contract was sold by the tiny but influential Memphis label Sun Records, where he had done his early and best work, to the monolithic RCA in New York, it was just the ducktailed tip of the iceberg.

Elvis went on to place ten songs in the top twenty in 1956 and was immediately whisked away to Hollywood, stuffed, bronzed, and packed into a time capsule. But in his wake came a motley army of uncivilized country types just aching to be loosed upon the charts. Carl Perkins, author of "Blue Suede Shoes," whose own version of the song outstripped Elvis's by a virtual country mile, was from Elvis's old label, Sun, which also spawned Jerry Lee Lewis, Johnny Cash, and Roy Orbison. He wasn't around the scene to enjoy the success of his song, however, as he was laid up most of that spring from a severe car accident which killed his brother. Gene Vincent had to journey from Norfolk, Virginia, to Los Angeles on a gimpy leg, with his group, the Blue Caps, to compete in an Elvis sound-alike contest, probably one of thousands of such contests being conducted in boardroom and basement as "the Pelvis" ascended his throne. Vincent won it with a song called "Be-Bop-a-Lula," which then went top ten.

While the country types singing rockabilly were making their inroads on the charts, the r&b veterans were still downstairs suffering the interrogation of the doorman in the lobby. Pat Boone took on Little Richard twice in 1956, splitting the pair. His version of "Tutti Fruiti" outsold Richard's, but Richard fared better on "Long Tall Sally." Bill Haley, no longer the only white hope, also had a battle with Little Richard, the Macon, Georgia, dishwasher, on "Rip It Up," which Richard won handily. Poor Haley, winded and pushing thirty years of age, couldn't even hoist the song into the top twenty. The Fontane Sisters fought off the Chordettes' cover of their own cover song, "Eddie My Love," in addition to fighting off the original, as sung by the Teen Queens. But Frankie Lymon & the Teenagers topped both the Diamonds and Gale Storm on his own "Why Do Fools Fall in Love," a top-ten hit.

Of all black groups, only the Platters, with their top hat and white tie and tails arrangements, could make the top of the charts in 1956 (they did it twice, with "The Great Pretender" and "My Prayer"). Yet there were encouraging signs of a break in the color bar at the lower rungs. Fats Domino managed a second-place finish with "Blueberry Hill." "Love Is Strange" by Mickey & Sylvia (written by Bo Diddley under his wife's maiden name), "Since I Met You, Baby" by Ivory Joe Hunter, "Treasure of Love" by Clyde McPhatter, "Jim Dandy" by LaVern Baker & the Gliders, and "My Blue Heaven" by Fats again, all landed in the top twenty, while "Let the Good Times Roll" by Shirley & Lee, "Fever" by Little Willie John, "In the Still of the Night" by the Five Satins, and "A Casual Look" by the Six Teens very nearly got there.

Not that the entrenched majority was about to jump off any bridges. However, by midyear the McGuire Sisters, aided and abetted by Lawrence Welk, were singing the "Weary Blues." A few months later Detroit's Guy Mitchell (real name, Al Cernik), one of Mitch Miller's prodigies at Columbia Records, started "Singing the Blues." By all lights a modest pseudo-country lament, this song spent ten weeks at Number 1 in *Billboard*, becoming not only the top song of the year, the top song of the *decade,* but, according to one research source, "the top song of *all time!*"

Take that, rock 'n' roll.

.■

*B*y 1957 the tide seemed to be shifting in favor of the young contender, rock 'n' roll. Rather than gracefully bowing to the inevitable and retiring from the Top 40 to the lucrative hotel-lounge deals awaiting them in Miami and Las Vegas, the deacons of pop's elite had one last joker up their sleeve. Seizing upon Harry Belafonte's easy-going calypso tune "Jamaica Farewell," which had done moderate business late in 1956, those in pop power pulled out all the stops by importing virtually every big gun in the casino to ride this baby calypso home a winner and divert the heads of the audience steadily coming under the influence of rock 'n' roll. No less than six heavies had renditions in 1957 of "The Banana Boat Song." There were the folkish Tarriers, featuring Alan Arkin on banjo, who put it in the top five. Harry Belafonte, of course, had his own version out. So did Steve Lawrence and Sarah Vaughan. Even the Fontane Sisters decided they had a thing for the sounds of the islands. Stan Freberg's satirical edition of the same song, released in March, was no doubt intended not only to sum up but also to write *finis* to the madness.

No such luck. 1957 was literally awash with these melancholy and escapist sentiments, put forth by pop music's finest. Thus, Tony Bennett sang "In the Middle of an Island," Rosemary Clooney gave us "Mangos," and the Four Coins yearned for "Shangri-la." Both the Hilltoppers and Terry Gilkyson (once of the Weavers) & the Easy Riders idolized that island girl "Marianne." (The flip side of the lamentable "Darling, It's Wonderful," by the Playmates that year, was the equally lamentable "Island Girl.") Don Rondo's "White Silver Sands" made the top ten easily. Roger Williams made the top fifteen with the instrumental "Almost Paradise," a song that was covered by no less an influential and tasteful personage than Norman Petty and his trio. (Norm had not as yet struck it rich with his protégé Buddy Holly.) Old Harry Belafonte didn't do too badly himself, hitting big with "Mama Look a Bubu," "Island in the Sun," and "Cocoanut Woman." All this intense calypso action eventually led to the emergence of the Kingston Trio (named after Kingston, Jamaica), whose "Tom Dooley," a Number 1 song in 1958, gave the barons of pop the folk boom, another soft, peaceful retreat from the cannons of rock 'n' roll.

However, in 1957, this rock 'n' roll audience was proving not quite as dumb as some had assumed. They were faithful to their Elvis. They sided with Chuck Berry when he sang "Rock and Roll Music." Calypso was big all right, but it just didn't have the same kind of cultural clout as the homegrown sound. So, ever sensitive to popular opinion, the establishment sent in its Hollywood troops to undermine rock 'n' roll from the inside. Trim, tanned, and stiff as billboards, these spiffed-up youngsters from TV and movieland proceeded to play good old country rock 'n' roll almost to a standstill for the rest of the season.

There was some substance behind the confusion. Take Elvis, at first glance the defending champion. In the blink of an eye he'd been snatched up by Hollywood—riding in limos, eating steaks. Suddenly his archrival Pat Boone, with his white bucks and pimple cream, didn't look so bad. Through the year they went at it like the Yanks and the Dodgers (the latter also soon to be taken by Hollywood, that great devouring menace to the young and the funky). Elvis had three of the top-five songs of the year, "All Shook Up," "Jailhouse Rock," and "Let Me Be Your Teddy Bear." Pat had the other two, "Love Letters in the Sand" (subtle bow toward calypso) and "April Love." Elvis thrust with "All Shook Up," Pat parried with "Don't Forbid Me," both also making Number 1. While Elvis's songs were supposedly delivered with unceasing animal lust and abandon, Pat's were refined and God-fearing, models of self-control. Rarely in the history of the popular arts has there been such a well-defined clash of mortal opposites, of Good (Pat) and Evil (Elvis). Or so it would have seemed, except for the creeping suspicion that both men were actually on the same side, both Hollywood playactors mugging for posterity.

For the real battle you had to look to the trenches, where rockabilly was going one on one with Tin Pan Alley West. Sonny James went at it with Tab Hunter on "Young Love." Both of them hit Number 1 with the song, but Hunter's version stayed up there for six weeks, while James was kicked out after one. Buddy Knox hit with "Party Doll" and Eddie Cochran made it with "Sittin' in the Balcony." But so did Debbie Reynolds with "Tammy." Sal Mineo and Tommy Sands both made the top ten, the former on "Start Movin'," the latter with "Teenage Crush," two songs which did their part in making a lot of lonely Saturday nights even more unbearable for those of us stranded in radioville.

Then again, 1957 was the year in which Jerry Lee Lewis, Buddy Holly & the Crickets, and the Everly Brothers all debuted on the charts, splitting six top-five records, some of the most enduring rock 'n' roll of the Top 40 era: "Whole Lot of Shakin' Going On," "Great Balls of Fire," "That'll Be the Day," "Peggy Sue," "Wake Up Little Suzie" and "Bye Bye Love." Concurrently, however, Frank Sinatra, Perry Como, Andy Williams, Steve Lawrence, Frankie Laine, and the Ames Brothers had *seven* in the top five that year: "All the Way," "Round and Round," "Butterfly," "Party Doll," "Moonlight Gambler," "Melodie D'Amour," and "Tammy."

And this is not even counting TV's own resident ticket on the sweepstakes, Ricky Nelson of "Ozzie and Harriet" ill-repute, who had three top-five items himself that year: "A Teenager's Romance," "Be Bop Baby," and "I'm Walkin'." At least Ricky was young enough to empathize with some of the experiences rock 'n' roll was documenting; but wasn't his own experience the antipathy of down-in-the gutter, spontaneous rock? Nevertheless, and be that as it may, he was a good deal more convincing than another youngster, Paul Anka, who exhibited his hotel-lounge aspirations right at the beginning with "Diana." (But if youth alone were the only prerequisite for Top 40 success, how do you explain the pubescent Brenda Lee, thirteen-going-on-thirty-one, whose "One Step at a Time" finished its mediocre run outside the Top 40, a notch behind David Rose's possibly haunting "Calypso Melody"?)

The year might have been a draw, a standoff, were it not for the unrelenting and increasingly visible presence of so many indomitable black groups. In fact, by this time the phrase *rhythm and blues* had become, in many white minds, synonymous with rock 'n' roll. That is, if an artist was acceptable to the mass (read *white*) market, he was considered rock 'n' roll. If he was as yet underground he remained r&b. Thus, where Jimmy Reed was the essence of rhythm and blues, Chuck Berry had "crossed over" to the lucrative land of rock 'n' roll. (This is a particularly vicious labeling game that has plagued black artists. Even before there was something known as rhythm and blues, all black singers were labeled "jazz," while similar white singers were allowed into the "pop" mainstream. Nat Cole, Billy Eckstine, and those of like color had to labor in the limited realms of jazz; Frank Sinatra, Tony Bennett, and Tony Martin worried not about admittance to the club. Elvis Presley, the king of rock 'n' roll, debuted singing the blues. The Beatles, his successors, made their reputation by reviving the works of such rhythm and blues stalwarts as Chuck Berry and the Isley Brothers.) The pop community, busy fending off the invading country rebels on the right, had little energy left over to deal with the durable black forces surging up from underground.

Led by Chuck Berry and Fats Domino, the blacks marauded the top ten in 1957. You had the Coasters with "Young Blood" and "Searchin' "; Little Richard with "Keep A-Knockin' " and "Jenny Jenny." Larry Williams did "Short Fat Fanny," a song which Pat Boone somehow failed to cover. The Dell Vikings (an interracial group) did "Come Go with Me" and "Whispering Bells." How about the Tune Weavers on "Happy Happy Birthday Baby," or Johnnie & Joe (from the Bronx) with "Over the Mountain, Across the Sea."

Not only had the top ten opened up, but the other thirty numbers, either as a bow to their genius, a nod to their persistence, or strictly as a matter of cash under the table, became increasingly available to a goodly bunch of pretty deep rhythm and blues characters, including Roy Brown (coiner, back in 1948, of the historic, "I heard the news, there's good rockin' tonight"), who made the charts with "Let the Four Winds Blow"; Jimmy Reed, author of "Big Boss Man" and "Ain't That Lovin' You Baby," landed in the Top 40 with "Honest I Do"; blues shouter Ruth Brown (no relation to Roy) made her first appearance on the charts with "Lucky Lips" (written by Leiber & Stoller); and Chuck Willis guided blues tune "C. C. Rider" to a good six months on the list.

Cover battles between blacks and whites were still going on, of course, but in most cases it was the black original winning the contest. Sam Cooke, for instance, over Teresa Brewer on "You Send Me," and the Rays (never to be heard from again, however) over the Diamonds on "Silhouettes." But the Diamonds did regain a measure of their self-esteem with "Little Darlin'," which they copped from the Gladiolas.

As an interesting sidelight to the whole cover record syndrome, a war gradually approaching an uneasy truce as 1957 echoed into oblivion, consider the black pianist Billy Ward and his group, the Dominoes (where Clyde McPhatter and Jackie Wilson got their start). In 1957 they put out their own covers of two of white America's most revered pop standards, "Stardust" and "Deep Purple," both of which made the top twenty.

Take that, pop music.

YEARBOOK 1958

.▪

*H*aving handily disposed of the pop-music beast, having at last achieved a bit of integration on the charts for its black citizens, and having firmly entrenched itself in the inner ear of the populace, rock 'n' roll, in 1958, proceeded to go soft. It was as if all these rowdy country boys had been suddenly civilized by their entry into polite society, as if all these urban no-accounts had been humbled by their popular acceptance. One by one our Top 40 stalwarts turned to the sentimental ballad to express their inmost feelings. One by one the black performers, up from r&b and gospel, sank to their knees to thank God for their good fortune. It was enough to drive the AM radio addict to folk music.

For the record, however, some of the most beloved rock 'n' roll ever to make the Top 40 was produced in 1958. Or was it just that we were all in the throes of puberty then, and particularly vulnerable to puppy love in its most abject guises? Certainly the leaders of the record labels were aware of this, as they released song after song devoted to reveling in the sordid details of this dangerous age and the subculture surrounding it. By and large bereft of similar details from any other source, it is understandable how the puberty-bound would devour this information, even then to write it themselves.

Sharon Sheeley was just such a teenager, lusting after Elvis at fifteen, and writing down her tales of torment in her room

23

in Newport Beach, California, late at night. One of them she showed to a new neighbor of hers, ten miles down the road in Laguna Beach. His name was Ricky Nelson. He put "Poor Little Fool" on his album; it came off the album as a single, and Sharon Sheeley became the youngest girl to ever write a hit song (whereupon she dropped out of school, moved her family to a penthouse apartment in Hollywood, got a tutor, bought a convertible and a little poodle, dyed her hair platinum, and signed a long-term staff-writing contract with Liberty). With real teenagers like Sharon writing on the West Coast (her boyfriend, Eddie Cochran, became her inspiration, sang all her demos; after his death her demo band consisted of Leon Russell on piano, Glen Campbell on guitar, and David Gates on bass), and on the East Coast Carole King and Neil Sedaka entering the fray, it wasn't long before we were getting epics of pubescent fantasy, unrequited love, lust, and hunger, with the occasional beach party thrown in to relieve the tension.

Basically written by girls about guys singing about girls, to be sung by a guy (and mainly bought by girls), the Top 40 in 1958 was beset with the sweat and pimples of adolescent life at its rawest (although the sounds themselves were mostly quite tame). Through this weird mirror we viewed what passed for romance in "All I Have to Do Is Dream" by the Everly Brothers, "Just a Dream" by Jimmy Clanton, "Little Star" by the Elegants, summed up by "It's Only Make Believe" by Conway Twitty. The Ponitails lamented they were "Born Too Late"; the Monotones sought advice from "The Book of Love." Even Elvis was frustrated in "Don't," and vulnerable in "I Got Stung." Dion & the Belmonts observed the situation with typical street-punk bravado in "I Wonder Why," effectively diminishing Paul Anka's pompous "You Are My Destiny." As Tommy Edwards counseled in "All in the Game," many a tear has to fall, to which Jackie Wilson in "Lonely Teardrops" and Little Anthony & the Imperials in "Tears on My Pillow" would undoubtedly add their amens.

So, while rock 'n' roll vixens like "De-de Dinah" (Frankie Avalon), "Jennie Lee" (Jan & Arnie), "Susie Darlin' " (Robin Luke), "Donna" (Richie Valens), and the immortal "Jo-ann" (the Playmates) called the tunes (certainly catchy and diverting, but they were just neighborhood girls after all; none of us had been exposed to such international types as "Ruby Tuesday," "Layla," and the immoral "Lola"), the suffering teenage guy on the street found solace in thoughts of cars, rebellion, summer vacation, and rock 'n' roll itself. He could idolize Chuck Berry's "Johnny B. Goode." He could empathize with the Coasters in "Yakety Yak." He knew what the Playmates were talking about in "Beep Beep." And "Summertime Blues" by Eddie Cochran hit him where he lived—bored, hurting, and broke, August on the brain.

Rock 'n' roll might purport merely to catalog the changing partners, fads, flings, whims of teenage life, but inevitably it gave you glimpses of the desolation. Danny & the Juniors could promote high school dances with a fervor in "At the Hop," the Diamonds jumped on the bandstand with "The Stroll," Bobby Freeman may have come on a bit too much like that one kid in every school who *really* knows how to dance in "Do You Wanna Dance," and Bobby Darin milked the last living sap out of those dreary encounters in "Queen of the Hop," but sooner or later you knew rock 'n' roll would have to get down, have to face the truth. The reality was finally revealed in 1960 by Bobby Bland in "Let the Little Girl Dance," a pathetic tale of wallflower and shy guy hopelessly separated by the insensitive and inchoate lindying throng, roadblocked, disconnected, doomed to spend the remainder of the weekend alone, listening to the radio, fantasizing, dreaming, and wishing on a star.

Wishing, perhaps, for some respite from the turmoil, "The Purple People Eater," "The Chipmunk Song," "Witch Doctor," "Western Movies," and "Splish Splash" were nothing more than Saturday morning cartoons, but as such they succeeded admirably. The Crests celebrated the age in "Sixteen

Candles." Chuck Berry's "Sweet Little Sixteen" was less about the age than the Age—the Age of Rock 'n' Roll. January was not too early in the year for Danny & the Juniors to reassure their constituents that "Rock and Roll Is Here to Stay," none among them wondering if they weren't perhaps protesting their case a bit too much.

Yet rock 'n' roll also knew that all such dreams were doomed, like the recurring summer dream alive in every schoolkid's impatient countdown to July, as epitomized by "Summertime Summertime" by the Jamies, a wonderful promise of freedom rarely fulfilled. Because if "One Summer Night" by the Danleers was the essence of summer love, encapsulated in a kiss on a porch swing, "Get a Job" by the Silhouettes was the comeuppance, the perfectly merciless morning after.

Tasting the heady wine of success in 1958, rock 'n' roll might have fallen a bit into some of the same easy patterns that had reduced pop music to so much airy persiflage, still it maintained the capacity to look at itself. Which is nothing to be sneezed at. Nevertheless, by April Fats Domino would be "Sick and Tired" and Chuck Willis would be dead in a car crash, having decided only a month earlier to "Hang Up My Rock 'n' Roll Shoes."

Did Chuck and Fats know something we didn't?

"Little Star"
(1958)
By the Elegants
■
VITO PICONE

"**N**obody had any bucks. There was a struggle. The next thing we knew we were on top of the world. I was in my last year of high school at the time, so I left to go on. Frankie left, he was a junior; Jimmy had graduated, Carmen had quit. We never really thought about any kind of financial situation at that point. We were just enjoying ourselves.

"We were on the road with police escorts, screaming fans and stuff, traveling all over the country. We played just about every state, including Hawaii, which wasn't even a state yet. We got very close with Dion & the Belmonts. Because we were on the road so long, we didn't know the extent of anybody else's hit record. We didn't know that Frankie Avalon, say, was beginning to mushroom into a bigger star than Bo Diddley. Backstage everyone was just doing his own thing. One tour was twenty-one days, one was ten days, one was a week, and they just kept flowing into each other. We would come back from one to find there was another one booked, or we would get sent a telegram that we had to appear at such and such place, and we would wind up there and someone would meet us and set up the next tour.

"That much touring was probably our downfall. We were on the road so long we didn't know we should have come back to New York and recorded the follow-up to 'Little Star.' We never really prepared for the second hit. We had a manager, but he wasn't really experienced either, to say the least. He was on the road making money, we were making money, and that's what he thought we should be doing. Nobody remembered that it all started in the studio.

"It was more than a year before we got back, and by that time the song had been well done, not only by us, but by other groups, like the Mystics, who did 'Hushabye,' simulating the sound. Everything we did from that point on was an imitation of 'Little Star.' We dug a ditch for ourselves. We went from Apt Records to United Artists and they wanted the same thing, another 'Little Star.' So we dug ourselves in a little deeper. Wherever we went, it just kept getting worse.

"Then the army came along and two of the fellows got drafted and they wound up going. Another one got married. I had an accident and was laid up for about six months. That was enough to separate the five of us long enough so that we realized it was just about all over with. Carmen got out of the business completely. Artie did also. Frankie and myself and Jimmy tried various things, but nothing really worked. I finally got out of the business, too, after about eleven years, at age twenty-eight.

"I only sing now on weekends and try to limit it as a hobby. I don't want to get reinvolved. I don't want to travel, that's for sure. I've got a decent position now, responsibilities, family, and what not. I really can't afford to make any moves. We're going to be playing soon at the Beacon Theater on Broadway. It'll be our third time there. It's a good feeling seeing a couple of thousand people sitting out there, still calling you by your first name. It's a good feeling even though it's twenty, twenty-one years later."

YEARBOOK 1959

▪▪

*I*n 1959 rock 'n' roll, as a sideline, went into the teenage idol business. At record labels big and small, national and local, the assembly lines were humming overtime, cranking out young, preferably white, preferably male, homogenized proto-types—affable, spit-shined, and conservative descendants of Uncle Pat. Some had been on the scene since way back in 1958, others were literally plucked off the street and trans-formed overnight into sex symbols. The packaging capacity that had only been hinted at by the Hollywood moguls in 1957 came to absurd fruition in 1959 in Philadelphia.

Off the conveyor belt and straight to Dick Clark's "Ameri-can Bandstand" program they went, lip-synching their way into the heart, soul, and pitter-pattering feet of impressionable pubes everywhere. Bobby Darin had talent, Frankie Avalon had charisma, Fabian had dimples, Bobby Rydell had . . . ? It was enough to drive Jerry Lee Lewis to drink. And it was enough to cause one Robert Zimmerman to quit playing piano in Bobby Vee's backup band, change his name to Bob Dylan, and head out in search of Woody Guthrie, some sort of authenticity out there beyond the jukebox.

As far as authenticity went, the rock 'n' roll audience had

gone in four years from the relatively ominous partying of "Rock Around the Clock" to the mewling bathos of "A Teenager in Love" by Dion & the Belmonts. And why not? All of these newly minted teen idols were singing their love songs for the same girl! The year 1959 saw a virtual National League pennant race for the favors of a Mouseketeer named Annette.

In addition to Avalon ("Venus" and "Bobbysox to Stockings"), Fabian ("I'm a Man" and "Tiger"), and Rydell ("Kissing Time" and "We Got Love"), hot in pursuit were Carl Dobkins, Jr. ("My Heart Is an Open Book"), Freddy Cannon ("Tallahassee Lassie"), Jan & Dean ("Baby Talk"), Skip & Flip ("It Was I"), and Travis & Bob ("Tell Him No").

Annette herself came out in favor of "Tall Paul." But was this song a wry put-down of the stocky Paul Anka, who was much too preoccupied being a "Lonely Boy" and socking the millions away to even partake of the hunt? Or did it instead allude to the more rangy Paul Evans, out of Columbia University, author of Bobby Vinton's later smash "Roses Are Red"? If so, we will have to forgive Evans if he didn't pick up on this invitation, since he more than had his hands full chauffering those "Seven Little Girls (Sittin' in the Back Seat)," all of them undoubtedly hungry for Annette's leftovers.

There were some moments of even greater import in 1959 than the soap opera of Annette. Astute listeners would sit up all night waiting for the foghorn in Frankie Ford's "Sea Cruise," or the incredible high-note finale by Janet Vogel of the Skyliners in "Since I Don't Have You." It was the year that "sha-bop sha-bop" entered the language via the Flamingos' version of "I Only Have Eyes for You." By accident we were given one of the oddest Top 40 hits of all time (and one of the funniest), "Say Man" by Bo Diddley, the result of a wily engineer leaving the tapes rolling during a particularly sassy exchange between Bo and sideman Jerome Green. In New Jersey the Fiestas brought back visions of 1955 r&b with "So Fine," and in Detroit the Falcons did the same with "You're So Fine." And if you had to have a song about sixteen, you could do worse than go with "Only Sixteen," a tune that would be revived years later by such notorious lechers as Ringo Starr and Dr. Hook, and sung at thirty-five with even more passion and desperation than the young Sam Cooke had originally imbued in it at twenty-four.

But the peak of 1959, one of the supreme radio moments in history, was Tommy Facenda's encyclopedic "High School USA," a song which consisted solely of the names of the actual high schools in at least forty of the major markets. Imagine the perspicacity of the guy (now a fireman in Portsmouth, Virginia), releasing forty different versions of the same idea (some collectors say as many as forty-six, although none has succeeded in collecting the *set*)! For all Facenda's efforts and ingenuity, however, the best the song could achieve was a paltry Number 28. Be true to your school indeed!

Despite "High School USA," despite the voluptuous Annette (today doing peanut butter commercials), despite the clean teens of "American Bandstand" and a few gems of r&b, 1959 was a murderous, dues-paying year for the kid, rock 'n' roll. It was hardly February when Buddy Holly's plane went down with Richie Valens, Peggy Sue, Donna, and The Big Bopper. Elvis was in the army. Little Richard had retired. Because he'd married his fourteen-year-old cousin, Jerry Lee Lewis was considered too immoral to be played on the radio. The government was about to put the crunch on Alan Freed. Thomas Wayne summed it up in "Tragedy." In March Tommy Dee's memorial to Buddy, Richie, and J.P., "Three Stars," went top twenty. In November Buddy came back, figuratively, in "Teen Angel" by Mark Dinning. And all through the year his ghost could be perceived (the ghost of rock 'n' roll itself?) hovering over the many tunes of doom that teenagers took to their hearts in 1959. There he was with Marty Robbins, high on a hilltop overlooking "El Paso," only to die a scant fifty yards from Rosa's Cantina. There he was again, pleading for his life in "Stagger Lee" by Lloyd Price. If you didn't notice him in Johnny Preston's Cherokee Romeo and Juliet saga,

"Running Bear," written by J. P. Richardson, a.k.a. The Big Bopper, maybe it's because he was moving too swiftly.

Is it any wonder the mobile troops remaining in the game were rushing headlong for the safety of the middle of the road? When Bobby Darin donned a tux and crooned his way to Vegas with "Mack the Knife," and the Drifters added a string section (previously anathema to bedrock rock and r&b) to "There Goes My Baby," you could almost see the white flags in their eyes. But as Buddy Holly himself indicated in his farewell lament (penned by pop prodigy Paul Anka), summing up from the middle of the road the music, the era, the struggle, "It Doesn't Matter Anymore."

"Come Softly to Me"
1959
By the Fleetwoods

∎

GARY TROXEL

"*B*arbara had a little Nash Metropolitan and we'd cram a whole bunch of people in that thing and just ride around drinking and making up songs. 'Come Softly to Me' was written for an Olympia High [Washington] talent assembly. It went over pretty well. Everyone said, 'You should record that.' Gretchen was dancing at a nightclub in Seattle, and the owners of the club introduced her to some people who wanted to form a record company. She played 'Come Softly to Me' for the people and that's how it started. We ended up driving to Seattle and recording that thing about ninety times over the course of three months just to get one good take.

"We worked pretty slow, pretty quiet. People at work still say, 'Here comes Mr. Rock and Roll.' I say we never sang rock 'n' roll. I think we were at the beginning of a change. One reason we made it like we did was that we were a kind of relief from all that noise.

"After the song hit, I don't know about the two girls, but as far as I was concerned, everybody found out who I was. People I didn't know would talk to me on the street. They'd say, 'Hi, Gary.' It was funny. I guess I'm kind of introverted. I didn't like meeting all those new people. Overall, I think, we were pretty turned-off to the music business. Most of the performers were okay, but I'm talking about the promoters of the different shows. The big names were fine, but it was all the little guys in all the little towns you had to watch out for. When we'd go on tour and be away from home for a while, I was always the one who was homesick, who wanted to get away from the hustle and bustle of that life. Gretchen loved it; Barbara was in the middle.

"The most vivid experience I have is of 'The Ed Sullivan Show.' When we got there the first thing they say is that we can't sing our whole song. We have to cut it down to a minute and fifteen seconds. That really unnerved me, because that's all we've been doing is singing the whole song. Now we had to cut out two verses. They dressed us up in cowboy outfits. The whole thing was a farce. We only had one microphone, which was way up in the air in front of me, so the two girls, who always sang behind me, couldn't even be heard. Then they added music to it. They had the whole band playing and everything was drowned out.

"I think that if I hadn't been in the navy, or signed up to go, things might have been different, but that's the way it happened. I had joined the naval reserves when I was in high school, just before we started singing together, so I was stuck. By the time I got out of the navy the big popularity thing had dropped quite a bit. That surprised me, because I was really close to the business. I was right there in San Diego, which is only 120 miles away. I was still cutting records with the group. The only thing I wasn't doing was going out on tour. I was replaced by Vic Dana.

"Since our record days we've had a lot of people phoning us and wanting us to record. What they want to do is take our time and sometimes our money, and then if it sounds good, if it does anything, we can have a contract. A couple of times we did it. But we always go into it thinking, would we disrupt our lives again for something like that if it happened? I think we probably would, because it's a way to get out of this life, the everyday, hour-by-hour jobs. But we sure would do a lot of things differently. The first thing we'd do is get a manager.

"We did some oldies shows in New York back in 1973, and one of the things in the contract was that they were going to meet us at the airport. We were all laughing about that, because we knew they weren't going to meet us. We laughed all the way there over the fact that they even offered to put it in the contract. So we got off the plane and waited around, waited around, and of course they're not there, so we didn't push it. But we thought, God almighty, this is just like the old days."

YEARBOOK 1960

■

*N*ow that they'd tasted the cuts of meat available on the supper club circuit (as opposed to the bologna sandwiches wrapped in cellophane on the locker room buffets of the high school hop route), rock 'n' roll's reigning crooners began to exercise their chops. Jackie Wilson gave us "Night." Elvis topped him in "It's Now or Never." Roy Orbison showed some lung in "Blue Angel." Dion & the Belmonts revealed their Broadway roots with "Where or When." The Skyliners covered "Pennies from Heaven." Ricky Nelson crooned "Yes Sir, That's My Baby." Everyone was turning to Tin Pan Alley for their inspiration. Both Connie Francis and Annette Funicello (now that she'd become eighteen she was entitled to a last name) turned to their native language, Italian, for "Mama" and "O Dio Mio," respectively. Several groups turned to the comics, including the Hollywood Argyles, with "Alley Oop," and the Ivy Three (two of whom, Charles Koppleman and Don Rubin, would one day own a record label), with "Yogi."

But all was not lost. While the Everly Brothers were signing with Warner Brothers for a cool million (and producing their final Number 1 single, "Cathy's Clown"), the Burnette Brothers, Johnny and Dorsey, were breathing rockabilly's last onto the Top 40 with "Dreamin'," "You're Sixteen" (Johnny), and

35

"Tall Oak Tree" (Dorsey), ably abetted by Wanda Jackson's "Let's Have a Party."

Meanwhile, anyone who was not running to Las Vegas was walking to New Orleans to look up Fats Domino, Al Hirt, and Huey Smith, author of the 1959 hit "Sea Cruise" by Frankie Ford, another resident. Freddy Cannon attempted to exploit the New Orleans consciousness (at the same time keeping both feet in the middle of the road) with the standard "Way Down Yonder in New Orleans." Gary U.S. Bonds was more emphatic with his own "New Orleans." Joe Jones defined the New Orleans Sound with "You Talk Too Much," as did Allen Toussaint, who began his producing career in 1960 with his job on Jesse Hill's "Ooh Poo Pah Doo," undoubtedly a mystic voodoo rallying cry, later to be updated by Mac Rebennack, otherwise known as Dr. John.

Whatever hardy souls remained, who neither walked to New Orleans nor ran to Las Vegas ("Walk—Don't Run" by the Ventures, went to Number 2 in 1960), were certainly dancing. Chubby Checker's letter-perfect cover of Hank Ballard's "The Twist" effectively took dancing from the cloistered world of the high school gymnasium into the garish reaches of the nightclub. Good-bye sockhop, hello discotheque. Taking dead aim on becoming the black Arthur Murray, Chubby next demonstrated "The Hucklebuck," and thereafter invented a new wrinkle on the twist nearly every fortnight. Hank Ballard wasn't resting on his laurels either. In May he gave us "Finger Poppin' Time" and in November "The Hootchi Coochi Coo." A new era of dancing was upon us, in the midst of which came Bobby Bland's impassioned cry, "Let the Little Girl Dance."

The little girl was not only trying to dance in 1960, she was breaking into song in record numbers. Up to then she had been shockingly light on role models. There was Connie Francis, but she was looking at Jo Stafford's tracks. Annette was a Mouseketeer! Connie Stevens, the girl to whom Edd "Kookie" Byrnes had loaned his comb in 1959, hardly possessed the stuff of a future spear carrier, let alone the pipes. Her "Sixteen Reasons" was saturated with a sensibility that was elbow deep in soapsuds. Wanda Jackson may have been feisty enough, but she didn't have the stamina for the long haul. Neither did Joann Campbell, who was restricted to novelty tunes depicting her as a harmless little girl, instead of the Blonde Bombshell we knew her to be. There were a few other "female Elvises" gadding about the countryside, untamed and willing, but none of them put it all together like Little Miss Dynamite. All of sixteen, all of five feet tall, Brenda Lee was part rockabilly, part country, part Judy Garland, and all trouper. She had played Vegas at eleven and headlined over Elvis at the Grand Ole Opry, as she would over the Beatles in Germany.

Maybe she was a bit too much of a trouper, though. As well as she could rock, she always covered her tracks with ballads. "I'm Sorry" and "I Want to Be Wanted" both hit Number 1 in 1960. And thereafter, if you were a rock 'n' roll woman you were welcome on the Top 40 only if you were also weak and docile, drunk with love, young, and innocent. In fact, Kathy Young & the Innocents (would you believe it?) led the way into this gauzy image of woman, with "A Thousand Stars." Rosie & the Originals were loyal with "Angel Baby." The Shirelles were submissive (but not entirely gullible) in "Will You Love Me Tomorrow." When the Crystals arrived with their homage to the male sex, "There's No Other Like My Baby," the father figures of the radio dial were still unaware of the demon energy they had accidentally tapped. For while Brenda Lee was dutifully "Rocking Around the Christmas Tree," there were others in her wake, in short skirts and spike heels and wearing eyeliner, whose experience was worlds away from Patience and Prudence.

These girls would take much of the play away from the boys throughout the early sixties—more than the piddling share they'd been accustomed to, anyway. Some of the best of them came from a particular neighborhood, a particular office building in Detroit, where ex–assembly-line worker Berry Gordy had begun to assemble his empire called Motown Records. It seemed like anyone who went to work for him as a secretary soon wound up with a top-ten record: the Marvelettes, Mary Wells, the Supremes, Martha & the Vandellas.

The first Motown Top 40 item was sung, however, by Barrett Strong. It was Gordy's thinly disguised plea for financial backing, "Money." Later in the year, as he began to get a foothold on immortality, began to sense that Motown was going to provide America with her best homegrown answer to the coming British invasion, Berry was insouciant enough to suggest that he could now affort to "Shop Around," a number cowritten with Smokey Robinson and brought to the top of the charts by Smokey and his group, The Miracles. Talk about miracles. Berry Gordy bought himself a bunch of charge-a-plates and a lot of heavy shopping ensued.

LUTHER DIXON

▪

Producer

"*A*fter I got out of the army I started singing background with a group named the Four Buddies. They had a hit called 'I Will Wait' on RCA Victor. I joined the group and we rehearsed for about six months on a special project and then the lead singer started drinking and he cussed out the head of A&R at RCA. So I said, well, the hell with this. I stopped singing, but I decided to learn the music business. I started off as a writer and after I wrote for a while I got into publishing and from publishing I became a record company owner. I started Scepter Records with Florence Greenburg.

"She had come to me to ask me to write a song for the Shirelles. I'd already written for Pat Boone, the Four Aces, Perry Como, and Nat Cole. I said, 'I'm giving my songs to top acts, I'm not going to give one to a small act. Florence said, 'Do it as a favor.' I did myself the greatest favor I could have done in my life. After I wrote 'Tonight's the Night,' with

Shirley, they said, well, we need a producer. I had produced a song called 'Sixteen Candles,' which was a hit by the Crests, so I said, all right, I'll produce it. Actually it was a guy named George Paxton, who was sitting with me in the control booth, who taught me what production was all about. We put a West Indian rhythm on 'Tonight's the Night,' because we knew there was a West Indian market in New York City, and they're the ones who bought the record first. I wanted to have strings, because r&b records weren't getting played on pop stations. I said, 'If I put in strings maybe it'll match the pop sound.' I put strings in the Shirelles' records. I put strings in Chuck Jackson's records and it began to work, and I got my pop play.

"I also did some background singing in studios, making demos for publishers. So I knew where the hits were. When I'd go to a publisher and tell him to play me some music, he knew I knew what he had. So I got good material. Then we'd get a pianist to come in and play the music while I rehearsed the Shirelles. I don't play an instrument. I went to school for theory, however. So I could tell the musicians what I wanted to hear and relate to them on musical terms. The communication was excellent.

"I had the responsibility to carry on that whole company. It was too much for me. I was overworked. So I left in 1962. I got into a deal with Capitol Records. Capitol owned 25 percent, Bing Crosby owned 25 percent, and I owned 50 percent. My first act would have been the Four Seasons. They had asked me to remix a record for them, and then I was supposed to get the record. The record was 'Sherry.' I wanted it for Capitol. I gave them a top deal. Then a guy by the name of Paul Marshall, on behalf of Vee Jay Records, at a convention in Miami, Florida, doubled my offer. So I lost the record.

"I just came back from Jamaica, where I've been living for ten years, working with writers there, really getting into the music. Reggae in Europe is just like r&b was in America when the white market began to buy black music. The attractive part of it is the political lyrics, because these Third World countries are all rebelling against their social structures. Now I'm ready to produce again. I'm producing Chuck Jackson. I'm remixing Bob Marley. I'm going to put what I learned into practice."

YEARBOOK 1961–1963

.▪

*F*rom January 1961 through October 1962 (unaccountably excepting August 1961), there was at least one dance record released per month that would ultimately reside on the Top 40, a total of forty-seven songs in all. And this is not even counting the songs that only talked about dancing, inspired dancing in their dominant beat, or implied the magical powers of dancing (such as "Do You Love Me?" by the Contours, in which it is suggested that dancing prowess alone could spell the difference between yea and nay in the mating game).

In January there was "Pony Time" by Chubby Checker and "Baby Sittin' Boogie" by Buzz Clifford. In February the Vibrations did "The Watusi." In March Hank Ballard & the Midnighters showed us "The Continental Walk." Chubby Checker was back in April entreating the weary to "Dance the Mess Around." In May the supple Gary U.S. Bonds danced until "A Quarter to Three." In June Hank Ballard did "The Switch-a-Roo" and the indefatigable Chubby Checker said "Let's Twist Again." Counter to this, in July Bobby Rydell tried "The Fish." In August everybody sat it out. But in September the Dovells brought forth upon the nation "The Bristol Stomp," and the Flares urged some "Foot Stomping." Chubby Checker discovered "The Fly" in October. In November Joey

Dee & the Starlighters immortalized their place of work, the Peppermint Lounge, in "Peppermint Twist." Even a street kid like Dion, who rather than dancing might have preferred getting caught doing homework or being nice to his mother, strutted his stuff in "The Majestic." Also in November, the inevitable Chubby Checker re-released "The Twist" (who said the Top 40 had no sense of humor?). In 1962 the number would scale the charts again, ushering in a year of dancing unprecedented in the annals of Terpsichore—but not before old Elvis closed out 1961 singing "Rock-a-Hula, Baby."

"Peppermint Twist"
1961
By Joey Dee & the Starlighters

▪

JOEY DEE

"We were at the Peppermint Lounge for exactly thirteen months, from September 1960 to mid-October 1961, when I wrote 'Peppermint Twist.' For the first nine or ten months the audiences were very sparse, but it was a great experience and a great place, because the people who did come in were super critical. If you weren't good they'd respond by throwing a beer glass at the bandstand. So you had to make sure you had your stuff together. From one night at the end of September 1961, I'd say it took about two weeks before the twist grew into a phenomenon.

"It was a once in a lifetime thing, to be lucky enough to be in the right place at the right time. You name them, they were at the Peppermint Lounge. I danced with Shirley MacLaine. I sat on her lap. Shirley was there every night. Judy Garland was there every night. Dorothy Kilgallen, John Wayne, Robert Mitchum, Liberace, a couple of senators, English royalty. On my wall I have gold records, platinum records, pictures with Muhammad Ali and Willie Pep. It's a great part of my past, but it *is* my past.

"We were on 'Bandstand' twenty times. We were the first band to be live on Dick Clark's coast-to-coast network show. We were given almost half an hour, and all we did was three songs. We only had a two-piece band, organ and drums—I occasionally played sax—but we were so confident once we started playing that we didn't need anything else. We did the Murray the K Christmas Show at the Brooklyn Fox, with Dionne Warwick, the Shirelles, Bob B. Soxx & the Bluejeans, and Johnny Maestro & the Crests. You were only on ten to fifteen minutes, and 'Shout' was fifteen minutes itself. Once we got involved in it the frenzy and momentum would carry it, and Murray would come out on stage and just keep it going, build it up to a climactic point, and then give me some kind of cue and we'd get off the stage. Backstage was a killer. You had a two-hour break. You'd hang out in the dressing room playing cards or trying to talk to some pretty chicks out the window. There was heavy security at the theater, but we'd be yelling out the window to them and they'd be yelling up to us, and we'd get a phone number or something. There were a lot of parties.

"Anybody I thought had talent, I'd let sit in with us. One time Ronnie Bennett, her sister Estelle, and her cousin Nedra sat in with us. They were charming, attractive girls, and the audience loved them. In the summer of 1963 we worked at a place called the Riptide, in Wildwood, New Jersey, for two weeks, commuting back and forth from New York. They sang background for us and were big hits, as I expected. Meanwhile in those two weeks, unbeknownst to me, Phil Spector was with them in the studio at four and five in the morning recording 'Be My Baby.' The record happened so fast that before our second week was out, on the way down in the car, we had the radio on and there's 'Be My Baby' by the Ronettes, and the whole thing happened for them.

"After a while I figured since I'd done club work all my life, it might be nice to own my own club. The grass is always greener, you know? But I lost money on it, not because the club was expensive to open and run, but because I got lazy and didn't go out on the road and work. We were one of the hottest groups in the country and the offers were phenomenal. The club was making it, but nowhere near what we could have made out on the road. We needed a house band. Dave Brigati, an original Starlighter, had gotten married and slipped out of the business. Dave's younger brother Eddie was a natural to join us since he knew our style and always used to sit in with us. Then I got Gene Cornish from a band that was breaking up in Rochester, New York, and Felix Cavaliere, who'd had a band called Felix & the Escorts. My new drummer was named Rick Channing, and they were my backup band at my nightclub, the Starlighter, right around the corner from the Peppermint Lounge.

"Finally Felix, Gene, and Eddie left the band and hired Dino Danelli, who I knew from the days of the Peppermint Lounge, when he worked up the street at the Metropole. They formed a group and started rehearsing out in the Hamptons. When they started to make it they came into the city and played at a place called the Phone Booth. At first they were known as the Young Rascals, then just as the Rascals.

"After I closed the club I put together another band. This time I got a fellow named Maurice James from Seattle, Washington, on guitar. Maurice James worked with me for a year; then he went to London and became Jimi Hendrix."

Like so many salted pretzels, the pop machine turned out approximately a dozen variations on the twist in 1962. The Marvelettes were first out of the gate with "Twistin' Postman." Sam Cooke was up "Twistin' the Night Away." Gary U.S. Bonds showed us the "Dear Lady Twist." Chubby Checker was only dogging it slightly in "Slow Twistin'." Joey Dee had a bright idea, "Hey Let's Twist," which was the title tune of a movie starring Jo-ann Campbell. King Curtis, whose previously impeccable sax credentials included all the Coasters' hits, fell in line with "Soul Twist." Gary U.S. Bonds returned, south of the border, with "Twist, Twist, Senora." The Chipmunks even did it in "The Alvin Twist." In May the Isley

Brothers added a new, shall we say, twist with "Twist and Shout." Jimmy Soul gave us "Twisting Matilda." A TV commercial was made into a twist, by Billy Joe & the Checkmates, "The Percolator Twist."

Yet there were a few staunch noncomformists out there who resolutely refused to twist. The Dovells tried to promote "The New Continental." Dee Dee Sharp announced it was "Mashed Potato Time." Nobody paid any attention. David Rose celebrated an entirely different kind of dancing with "The Stripper." Nobody got the joke. The Orlons did last season's "Watusi" one better with their own "The Wah Watusi." Then the Dovells came out in favor of "Bristol Twistin' Annie," signaling even their surrender to the craze. But Little Eva decided she'd rather do "The Locomotion." Chubby Checker gave a "Dancing Party," but Bobby Rydell wasn't invited, because he'd already sworn "I'll Never Dance Again." But when Chris Montez chirped "Let's Dance," the Dovells were back on the antitwist front lines with "Hully Gully Baby." Late that summer, perhaps speaking for the silent majority, the Shirelles cried "Stop the Music." But nobody was listening.

Certainly not Chubby Checker. In September he delivered not one, but two new dance steps to his exhausted minions, "Popeye the Hitchhiker" and "Limbo Rock." Whether "Popeye the Hitchhiker" is the same step as the Sherrys' "Pop-Pop-Pop-Pie," is a question that has baffled even "American Bandstand" regulars. To the naked eye, however, none of these dances and none of these records, seemed very much different from your basic twist.

Whatever. Lost in all this dancing were the hints of the next major cultural craze. The Mar-Kets tipped it off with "Surfer's Stomp," in January, which might have passed as just another dance. "Surfin' " by the Beach Boys was more explicit, but the song failed to make the Top 40, so no one knew about it, aside from the denizens of Pandora's Box in Los Angeles, where the Beach Boys, Jan & Dean, Dick & Deedee, and the rest of the L.A. music scene were extolling a more outdoorsy life-style. At the same time, Caesar & Cleopatra were growing their hair.

In a few more years they'd be ready to comb it, style it, change their names to Sonny & Cher, and become an industry.

"The Mountain's High"
1961
By Dick & Deedee
▪
DICK ST. JOHN

*"T*he Mountain's High' was released in the summer in San Francisco on a small label called Lama Records and it was an instant smash. I was still working; I had a little summer job passing out Viceroy cigarettes. Deedee was working at a candy shop. Within three weeks the record was Number 1 in San Francisco, and Deedee and I didn't even have a copy of it yet.

"When we first started getting booked, we were booked into a lot of black nightclubs, because in those days even with a hit record you didn't have any identity, you were just a sound. Within a year we started doing a lot of local shows with the Beach Boys, Jan & Dean, Glen Campbell, and Jerry Fuller. We played all sorts of high school assemblies. We toured constantly. We went about as many miles as any rock 'n' roll singer at that time could handle, mostly by car or bus. We wanted to make a lot of money, and the only way to make a lot of money was to work all the time, because the most you were picking up from any of these places was probably $250 a night.

"All in all we really enjoyed it. The atmosphere was always very warm. I can't remember anyone I ever met who was a rock 'n' roll singer from that era who wasn't loving and kind. I remember one time admiring Roy Orbison's shoes. He'd just come back from Australia and they were something special. So he said, 'Do you want them?' And he took them off and said I could have them. But he wore size eight and I wear size ten.

"There used to be Disc Jockey Appreciation Nights. Because they'd been so generous in playing your record all year, you would go and do a free show for them. They'd give a big party and it would be fun, and then, of course, they'd play your next record. Well, this one time in Texas we ended up back at the hotel and everybody was drinking and this deejay decided we'd have elevator races. It was an old building with two elevators that had little glass triangle windows in them and hand controls so you could make it go faster or slower, and stop at each floor; I think there were six floors.

"So this deejay pushed out the little old ladies who were running them, and we started these elevator races. We'd get in at the basement and go up to the roof and see who could go up and down the fastest. The deejay had hold of one elevator and he kept thinking he could beat the record. Meanwhile, everybody stood on the fifth floor, looking through the triangle windows where you could see the elevator going by real quick.

"I had done this a couple of times, but I was tired of it. Besides, it was making a lot of commotion. We didn't mind commotion, but it was getting a little out of control. The deejay was bombed. He said this was the last time and he was going to do it faster than he'd ever done it. He started at the bottom and just kept going really fast. He was out of his mind, happy, laughing, just having a great time. Then all of a sudden we heard the elevator kind of go *zzzzz*. The cord had broken. The deejay came by us on the fifth floor with a really pathetic look on his face. The control lever had come off in his hands.

"Anyway, he crashed in the basement in all this dust and dirt. We all ran down to get him. He had busted both his legs, but he was still out of his mind. Until the ambulance came and took him away he kept saying it was the greatest thing he'd ever done.

"I'm sure rock 'n' roll tours are still pretty much the same."

In November 1962, Steve Lawrence said "Go Away Little Girl," and suddenly that would be it for dancing for about ten years. (It was not until the early seventies, when boys started dancing with boys, that you had your next dance cycle.)

Steve was no doubt also commenting on the preponderance of females now staking claims on what was previously male turf. By 1962 they'd all but set up housekeeping, bringing their flowers, plants, drapes, and throw pillows to the bachelor pad of the Top 40. All these women certainly were enticing to the good old boys of rock 'n' roll. Down on the corner Bruce Channel tried his pickup technique with "Hey Baby." It didn't work. Don & Juan were more straightforward in "What's Your Name." Gene Chandler, in an effort to meet some chicks, dubbed himself the "Duke of Earl." Dion probably got the most action. Soon after dousing his torch for "Run-around Sue," he became "The Wanderer."

Tommy Roe was sweet on "Sheila." The Four Seasons called for "Sherry." But there were also Timi Yuro, Shelley Fabares, Hayley Mills, Barbara George, Linda Scott, and Carla Thomas. The Angels were still in business, as were the Shirelles, the Exciters, the Crystals, and the Blue Belles. Ann-Margret hit the charts in 1961. Rosie & the Originals were seasoned vets, as were Jo-ann Campbell, the Chantels, the Marvelettes, Cathy Jean & the Roommates, Rochelle & the Candles, and Patsy Cline.

By and large, however, the love life of these Top 40 ladies was horrid. They were open, vulnerable, and invariably stomped on. Connie Francis set the tragi-romantic tone in "Where the Boys Are." Cathy Jean & the Roommates were unspeakably naïve in "Please Love Me Forever." The Paris Sisters were merely blandly passive in "I Love How You Love Me." They had a long way to go before they'd achieve their sought-for emotional parity. Timi Yuro was "Hurt." Patsy Cline admitted "I Fall to Pieces," and later to being "Crazy." Collectively these women were tied to the personification of the macho man, whether he be "Johnny Angel," "Johnny Jingo," "Johnny Loves Me," "Johnny Get Angry," or "Norman." The Cookies were in "Chains." The Shirelles sat home waiting for a "Soldier Boy." The Blue Belles led the devotion derby in "I Sold My Heart to the Junkman."

Even though Timi Yuro was finally able to sneer "What's a Matter Baby?" when her old lover got kicked out of his new love's bed, and no less a figure of reserve and decorum than

Dionne Warwick demanded "Don't Make Me Over," these token protests were more than offset by the many acquiescing female voices. All Marcy Blaine wanted in life was to be "Bobby's Girl." The big thing for the Exciters was to "Tell Him" that they were never going to leave. So be it. But Little Eva was divisive in her warning "Keep Your Hands off My Baby." To find a more antagonistic sister you'd have to wait until 1963, when the snarling Lesley Gore arrived with "It's My Party."

All in all, it was a bad era for lovers of both genders. Either you spent it living from one "Lonely Saturday Night" to another, or you dropped out completely and climbed "Up on the Roof" to wait for the love generation to happen. If you entered the fray, at least you took heart in the litanies the Top 40 presented. Bob B. Soxx & the Bluejeans (with Darlene Love singing lead) wondered "Why Do Lovers Break Each Other's Heart." The Crystals (with Darlene Love singing lead) loved a bad seed in "He's a Rebel." Timi Yuro, so brave a few months ago, crumbled completely in 1963 with "Make the World Go Away." Brenda Lee concurred in "My Whole World Is Falling Down." And Skeeter Davis made them both cheer up with "The End of the World."

Sage Gene Pitney counseled "True Love Never Runs Smooth," to which Paul & Paula could only nod, having just experienced their "First Quarrel." Little Peggy March, who had publicly bucked the trend, declaring "I Will Follow Him," by August was hedging her bets with "Hello Heartache, Goodbye Love." And while Brian Wilson and the Beach Boys were hiding "In My Room" and Barry & the Tamerlanes were musing "I Wonder What She's Doing Tonight," Del Shannon was out searching for his "Runaway" and Roy Orbison was "Crying" (but ever so eloquently). Freddy Scott was just as wrenching in "Hey, Girl," while the Jaynettes were cryptic in "Sally Go 'Round the Roses." Less cryptic was Lesley Gore, again berating a fellow woman, in "She's a Fool."

The year that started with the Four Seasons being instructed to "Walk Like a Man" and ended with the Cookies advising

"Girls Grow Up Faster Than Boys" also had its more friendly moments between the sexes. Ruby & the Romantics were all sympathy in "Hey There Lonely Boy." The Chiffons were well satisfied in "He's So Fine," with a lyric espousing the virtues of the "soft-spoken guy." The Ronettes were unafraid in "Be My Baby." But the Cookies were a bit defensive in "Don't Say Nothin' Bad About My Baby." And the Angels were definitely counterproductive in "My Boyfriend's Back." On the other side of the coin, Barbara Lewis, in her mature, cool, but not uncaring "Hello Stranger," said volumes about the shortcomings of most teenage relationships. (If you wanted adult relationships, you listened to country music.)

Everyone else, still in high school, still trying to cope, went along with the Essex, who summed up the difficulties inherent in getting your body to go along with your mind, your impulses to coincide with your intuitions, and your feet to keep time to the music in "Easier Said Than Done."

"Sherry"
1962
By the Four Seasons
■
FRANKIE VALLI

"I really didn't get into rock 'n' roll until the late fifties. I was more jazz oriented. For a long time I was really bent on making it as a straight-ahead singer with a modern kind of group, like the Four Freshmen or the Modernaires. I was always stimulated by the big bands. It's an era I wish would come back.

"I worked with groups called the Varietones and the Four Lovers; I've recorded under the names of Billy Dixon and Frankie Tyler. I did some solo things under the name of Frankie Valli. They were whatever the current market called for, whatever was happening at the time. I did a lot of studio work, singing on demos for publishers. I heard all of Elvis's songs before Elvis did. The writer of all those songs like 'Don't Be Cruel' and 'All Shook Up' was this black kid out of Brooklyn named Otis Blackwell.

"When Bob Gaudio joined us we were one of the hottest groups in the New Jersey area; we'd played every lounge on the Eastern seaboard. We did a mixture of r&b, jazz, and middle-of-the-road-oriented material. After he joined the group we focused more on rock 'n' roll. He'd been one of the Royal Teens and he wrote all their hits. Anyone who can write from 'Short Shorts' to 'Can't Take My Eyes Off You' is a great writer. One day when we were getting ready to go in and cut some sides, he wrote 'Sherry' in about fifteen minutes before he left his house. He came to rehearsal with it and he said, 'I just wrote a smash, you have to learn this song.' We learned it right away and we went in and cut it. Shortly before that we'd changed our name from the Four Lovers to the Four Seasons to symbolize our new direction.

"In about three to four weeks we saw results. All of a sudden the record was Number 1. It happened so quickly that I don't think we realized what was going on until the fifth or sixth record. A lot of the promoters thought we were a black act, so we did a lot of all-black tours, including the Apollo Theater in Harlem. Certain parts of the country were not accepting that kind of tour, and there were some hairy moments. We were doing a tour with Chubby Checker, right in the midst of the Old Miss problems, and we were playing Jackson, Tennessee, at an armory where they were protesting. We had to cancel the show, pack up, lay down on the floor of the bus, and get out of town. I grew up in a major city; I lived in a mixed environment. I'd read about segregation, but I'd never experienced it before.

"In those days the artists cared about each other. The tours were family-oriented. There'd be ten acts, you'd go out for thirty days, and there'd be singing on the bus, and the talk that went back and forth, singing with the other groups, and whatever. It was a different kind of business. The egos were nothing like they are today. People were involved in the music business more for love than for money. Money has changed this business tremendously."

YEARBOOK 1964 (R.I.P.)

■

*I*n 1964 the Beatles started rock 'n' roll's second generation. The original seekers of the fifties, who sent their letters home on 45s, were forced to the sidelines of the Top 40, their bellies gone to fat, their good intentions gone to show tunes, still kids in the eyes of the world, but elderly in the young man's game.

Motown broke through in 1964, revealing a picture of black adolescent life that seemed essentially no different from white adolescent life—which may have been Chuck Berry's message all along. Neither was British life very far off the norm, perhaps because it was being scripted by some of our Tin Pan Alley veterans. California lit up briefly on the Top 40, luring us into the sun and surf—only to come up with Watts in 1965, bursting the bubble for good. And the women, those docile dollies tiptoeing through the man's world of the charts, in 1964 finally started tossing dishes against the wall. Lesley Gore started out the year raging "You Don't Own Me." By November she was musing "Sometimes I Wish I Were a Boy." Gale Garnett in "We'll Sing in the Sunshine" truly offered a harbinger of the new consciousness about to descend on the airwaves, rendering the staid Top 40 nearly obsolete.

New consciousness, new techniques (the blossoming of the Phil Spector Sound, one-half Leon Russell, one-half Darlene Love), new groups—and the only place you could count on seeing the old favorites was on TV. In 1963 on "Shindig" you might catch a glimpse of Jerry Lee Lewis and Little Richard (who had been coaxed out of retirement, imminently to retire again), but the show would be off the air by 1967, by which time FM radio would be the new cultural switchboard, and the album its favored mode of conversation.

The audience that discovered the Top 40 as teenagers in the mid-fifties were intent upon taking rock 'n' roll to college with them. A president shot down had united them in blood and rage. The folk music of the Kingston Trio and Peter, Paul & Mary had hardened into the folk rock of protest, music of the front lines. By 1967, when it traveled west to merge with the consciousness of the frontier, it would be known as acid rock. Although the Top 40 tried to present these changes ("Eve of Destruction" by Barry McGuire, "San Francisco" by Scott McKenzie, advising all young runaways to wear some flowers in their hair, "White Rabbit" by the Jefferson Airplane), as with its belated and watered-down recognition of rhythm and blues, by the time these songs surfaced on AM radio, they were already yesterday's news.

But what of those old friends, forgotten originators, bound and sinking with the ship of the Top 40? Like rock 'n' roll, they were forced to grow up, too. I found them confronting the age-forty crisis with these bleak and bizarre scenarios. Little Richard hustling Bibles. Chuck Berry in jail for tax evasion. Roy Orbison, a living legend, just barely, guesting in *People* magazine. Jackie Wilson hovers in the dark limbo between the false ending and the actual ending of Bobby Freeman's "Do You Want to Dance?" Encountered in a New York City hotel room, Bo Diddley is incomprehensible much of the time, the rest incensed. Denied the major share of the royalties due him, he is determined, as far as history goes, to get a proper accounting. "I was the originator," he says. "I don't hate Elvis Presley. I never have disliked him. But at one point I thought he could have gotten his own act and left mine alone." Presley himself, bug-eyed and slack-jowled at forty-two (the same age as John Coltrane and Lenny Bruce), is gone, expiring in Memphis from a diet of multicolored pills.

Jerry Lee Lewis, by all accounts, still relentlessly grinds on, but Jerry Lee is, of course, Jerry Lee.

Is there one of all the original holy voices who has remained unscarred by tragedy, undimmed by time? Is there one who has managed to cross that Rubicon of forty with style and finesse, ageless as Dick Clark?

"Stood Up"
1958
By Ricky Nelson

▪

The sign over the toilet backstage at the Broadway Theater in Pitman, New Jersey, reads: Do Not Flush During Show. Alongside the scrawled signatures of such country music perennials who've played the Broadway as Freddy Fender, the Oak Ridge Boys, the New Christy Minstrels, and Rick Nelson, the name Anita DeMarco is prominent on nearly every one of the dozen dressing-room walls, as well as the wall in the john. She may be the ultimate country music groupie, an inspiration to all the boys who do not flush during show. Or else, perhaps, a latter-day incarnation of the legendary Arline of Rick's childhood, the girl, it's been written, in quest of whose favors young Eric bravely began his recording career. Where is Arline now? Where is Anita? There are other, even more searching questions to be asked—for instance, where is Rick Nelson?

It is 7:00—showtime—but Rick has not arrived. Backstage the promoter, the stage manager, the cop brought in for riot control, and the house photographers—family men reeking of home cooking and vintage after-shave—mumble nervous jokes. They recall the way it was only last November when Rick Nelson canceled out on them, leaving the New Christy Minstrels to do a two-hour set, leaving the promoter about five grand in the hole. They are also aware that he had to bow out of the following night's show in Englewood, having failed to outdraw the Super Bowl on TV.

The opening act, Tony Santoro, a middle-aged, middle-of-the-road comedian, spit-shined black hair, tux, dancing pumps, takes the stage gamely at 7:15, prepared to do his act and a half, all the jokes he knows. At 7:25 the promoter is informed that Nelson and entourage are en route from the Philadelphia Airport. The relief is palpable; for a town like Pitman, Nelson is a major league attraction. But they may think twice before booking him again.

At 8:00 the caravan arrives, just as Tony Santoro is completing his third encore. The members of the Stone Canyon Band, grizzled roadmap veterans, troop downstairs, followed by Rick, impeccably coiffed and natty, on first impression looking much smaller than expected, but also, somehow, taller.

"He must be, what, thirty-five or thirty-six?" the uniform speculates.

"Forty," he is told.

"Clean living . . . ," the gendarme concludes in awe.

After Elvis, so the lists affirm, it is Ricky Nelson, teenage TV heartthrob, who racked up the best figures on the Top 40. While this position may be tarnished a bit by the captive audience his media exposure afforded him (as opposed to the glasses and bad teeth of Buddy Holly, or the glasses and bad everything of Roy Orbison), reconstructed critics point out in his favor the quality musicians like James Burton, the guitarist who later played with Elvis, who surrounded Ricky, tutored him, undoubtedly elevating his tastes well beyond the limits of his Hollywood roots.

Once he said that everything came easy for him; his TV career as a junior Jerry Lewis, his rock 'n' roll career as a three-chord superstar before he even played his first concert. But in the years since the fifties, when the hits stopped coming so fast, rising so high, and especially in the years since "Garden Party," that sweet top-ten vindication in 1972, things have seemed to become more difficult for Ozzie and Harriet's baby boy. For one thing, the country music audience can hardly be said to have clutched Rick to its bosom. His latest foray onto those charts, once considered a haven for aging, repentant rock 'n' rollers, was a whisper-soft remake of Bobby Darin's "Dream Lover," which failed to penetrate the down-home Top 40.

Barely half an hour behind schedule (a trifle in these days of superstar affrontery), Nelson and the Stone Canyon Band take the stage to a moderate ovation from the three-quarters house.

"We did better in November," mutters the still sweating promoter.

Nelson's guitarist has wired, punk-rock red hair, the keyboard man a wispy, Mandarin, knee-length, six-year-old fantastic goatee, admired by the cop backstage, who jealously wonders what it would look like aflame. They must, *must* have dirty lyrics for all of Rick's old standards that they sing to the stewardesses on the plane ride home, with Rick himself on high harmonies.

Onstage, however, in sequined flares, Nelson is much more low key. He jumps slightly to end every other song. What little he says to the audience is mumbled into his shoulder, swallowed in grimaces, tics, and shrugs. The audience, recalling him as a shy clown, giggles appreciatively. These are Ricky Nelson fans, as opposed to country music fans, as opposed to Rick Nelson fans. (The best way to tell that Rick is forty is by looking at the ladies in the audience, who've worshipped him since their teens, and his.) But you've got to hand it to him. Where he could have easily played this phase of his life Paul Anka suave or Elvis show biz, Rick chooses to rock out. He has compromised none of his ideals to country music, pop music, or old age. The classics sound every bit as genuine as they did when they were new. Maybe it's the influence of the band, but nevertheless, he's still living out the dream, even if his jeans are custom-made.

Thus he completes a neat, tight, semienergetic sixty minutes for what is perhaps the oldest audience ever assembled in one theater for a rock concert, some folks who haven't screamed so loud since "Ozzie and Harriet" went off the air in 1966.

After his obligatory encore, Nelson lopes offstage with the band and disappears downstairs. In less than five minutes the area begins to fill with his fans toting dog-eared glossies, dog-eared spouses in short leather car coats. He is presented with all sorts of ancient memorabilia, including one very fine mint-condition Ricky Nelson comic book, circa 1957, wielded by a stout lady of middle years in a bouffant hairdo. Stood up by Ricky Nelson in November, they now bulge toward the cop at the top of the stairs in the attempt to reclaim this idol of their youth.

In squads of six they are allowed into Rick's dressing room, to offer momentary flashbulb blindness and memorabilia for autographs. Like the star of the one-dollar-a-kiss booth at a hayseed carnival, the hostess at a dime-a-dance den up a flight in the city, Nelson endures the supplications of the locals with a glossy smile, his cocktail party banter soon dwindling to anxious small talk.

"Hi, Rick, say hello to Debbie. Debbie, come on in here, will you?"

"Hi, Debbie."

"She's just shy."

"Yo, Debbie."

Where Elvis, in order to avoid his admirers, acquired a string of bodyguards (each of whose bylines now graces an as-told-to exposé), Nelson, owing to light times, perhaps the energy and economy crunch, or his years separated from the flesh of his minions by cathode tubes and artificial scripts, employs no bodyguards, takes on his fans without benefit of future biographers. Some of them, however, know as much about him as any biographer might.

"Is it true you were dropped from Epic, Rick?" asks the stout lady, offering Nelson the comic book to sign.

"Uh, yeah . . ."

"But you were picked up by Capitol?"

"Uhmmm, right."

"And Capitol is going to be releasing an album of your old rock songs?"

"Uh, are they?"

"Anything to add to that, Rick?"

"Uh, nope."

When he was the King's runner-up, perhaps the small talk seemed much larger to Nelson. When the one-dollar-a-kiss booth was charging a steeper admission price, maybe the smile was less glossy. But would a brand-new run of top-ten smashes make this stout lady seem any less stout? She was probably just as vociferous during his first run, back in the fifties. And even if at one time this trip may have really been a jolt, how long can anyone expect to sustain such a high—first love—or even want to? (On the other hand, does it bother Rick that the lowliest member of the Eagles probably grosses more in a week than he will in a year of Pitmans?)

However, far from feeling sorry for the fallen idol denied the adulation of his youth, it's clear that for Rick Nelson this new plateau offers welcome relief from such multiplying hordes, a vacation for the singer in which he still gets to play, but without so much undue fanfare.

Although Neil Young may have stated a preference for burning out over fading away, Rick Nelson gets to do both.

Part
TWO
Singers

CONNIE DeNAVE

■

Publicist

"*9* got a job as Dick Clark's press agent in 1957. In 1958 I went out on my own with Fabian, Frankie Avalon, Connie Francis, Dion & the Belmonts, and Dick Clark as clients. I had desk space at Laurie Records under a filing cabinet; when the A–D drawer was pulled out, it would hit me on the head. In six months the business had grown so fast I had to move to a whole floor.

"The rock 'n' roll stars of the fifties were innocent and clean. They weren't sophisticated enough to articulate well, but the kids related to them because they were street types who'd worked their way up, singing music of the street. They may have lacked polish, but we gave it to them. We had to teach them social manners so they wouldn't feel insecure when they talked to the press. They would do interviews over lunch and all they would order were hamburgers. In my office were over a hundred menus, and I would teach them to order snails, lobster. In those days editors asked the same questions: What's your favorite color? What kind of girls do you like? Do you wear pajamas when you go to bed? It was all superficial teenybopper stuff, but remember, life in those days was superficial. We didn't get into heavy things like politics. So we prepared psychological responses to 285 questions and the acts were trained. Then the wardrobe. I would buy their clothes. Now managers do that, but in those days the managers were more naïve than the acts.

"I was called an image maker; the name of my company was The Image Makers. But the image was true-to-life. I wouldn't allow any drinking. I was never aware of any sexual activities. My kids stayed inside watching cartoons on TV. Pranks were very big in those days. The one or two who fell to drugs kept it quiet. If you drank or smoked in public you'd be ruined overnight, because parents would be outraged. A paternity case could destroy you. If you had a wife you were finished; it would ruin your career. Everyone was isolated then and I was an overprotective mother hen.

"There were big security problems. Dick Clark did the Hollywood Bowl one time. He had thirty convertibles to get all the acts back to their hotels. I had Fabian and Frankie Avalon in my car. The kids were all on cliffs in the backstage area. In those days if they loved you they'd toss things at you. Frankie got knocked out cold by a stuffed elephant. I got knocked out by some sort of steel statue. Our driver was knocked unconscious; one of our road managers jumped in and got us out of there, driving through about six hundred people. The car was filling up with toys and gifts and love letters. I was crying for about ten minutes. Another time I was at the airport with Fabian. The windows of the limo were closed and the oxygen was going, the driver couldn't move and the kids kept pounding on the glass. Finally the glass started exploding and it got Fabian in the eye. We were both in the hospital.

"Fan mail was very important. Hype was fun then. In the sixties they made it into a dirty word. My biggest thing was the fan magazines. Once in a while you'd get dignified. I remember *Esquire* doing something on Fabian in which they shot a picture of him with a Band-Aid on his face. I asked them why they did that. They said it was just for drama, his being hurt. But instead it turned out they were really trying to make it look like Fabian was covering a pimple.

"The big step was the transition from teenybopper to the Copa. At first the kids didn't have any ambitions, but when Paul Anka and Bobby Darin broke through they started a rush. I spent my days and nights at the Copa. That was my training ground.

"Financially the problems were all the same. The mother and father wanted a house, then dad needed another car. The fights would begin at home and the money would start going. Sister needed new teeth, then she wanted to go to college; she needed new clothes, then she was getting married. Let me tell you, their families were really big spenders.

"I've spent twenty years in rock 'n' roll and every day *Time* and *Life* told me it wasn't going to last. They just refused to accept it. 'The Twist' was Number 1 in America in 1960 and a year later it went back to Number 1 because that's when the media accepted it. Before that the media wouldn't dignify it with press coverage. When you got press it was amazing because you competed for very little space. Now there are whole entertainment sections.

"The record business today is a total joke compared to what it was in the fifties. In the fifties the simplicity of the business was magnificent. It was a seat-of-the-pants operation; guts and gambling made the business. When you wanted to find talent you rode the subways. When the subway doors opened up, you'd listen to hear if anyone was practicing in the station. There were no showcases like today. Today the record business is run by accountants, bookkeepers. In those days you spent $37,000 on a record and that was life and death. Now they spend a million dollars and don't blink an eye.

"The punk rock and new wave groups of the seventies are a community of loners, manifesting hostility and anger. In the sixties the Beatles had a great sense of humor. They hit at a psychological time of great mourning and they made America laugh. The timing was all of it. If they'd tried it in the fifties, no way. They were too sophisticated. Rock 'n' roll in the fifties was innocence."

THE FIVE SATINS

FRED PARRIS

◾

*T*he name Fred Parris seems fated to be bound forever with one song, "In the Still of the Night," one of the most enduring and evocative of the singles to bridge the channel from rhythm and blues to rock 'n' roll in 1956. It is at the center and along the perimeter of Fred Parris's story, a tale as old as rock 'n' roll, probably as old as rhythm and blues. Its chance creation defines his career, glorifies it, and limits it. He's never been able to duplicate that song's success, yet when he's tried to run and hide from it, the song has always found him. It's gotten him jobs when he's been down; it's lured him out of comfortable work. When the song first hit he was in no way able to take full advantage of the fame it might have offered. Even more to the point, he was to be denied the greater part of the riches it should have accrued. He has spent his life in the grasp of that song, going so far as to engage in legal action in the attempt to recover his due. And recently there has been a rumor that he never really wrote the song in the first place.

A not dissimilar fate befell many of the classic groups and writers from this supposed golden era of rock 'n' roll. It was a world populated by hungry footloose kids, dreamers, romantics, naïfs in the ways of big business. They just wanted to record their song, get it out, get it heard, and revel in the approval of their peers. It was obvious they didn't know about agents, managers, royalty statements, and the nuts and bolts (and screws) of a show business career. Rock 'n' roll to them was not a career at all—it was a lark, an accident. Some of the biggest groups of the era, the pioneers whose influence has reached second and third generations, whose records consistently made the charts, came away from their glory years bittersweet, unable to prove anything conclusively, to lay their hands on the necks of any culprits, and for all their success, curiously short of bankable funds.

In his hometown of New Haven, Connecticut, Freddy Parris entertained other dreams, mainly of curveballs and shutouts. Through high school he pitched with a variety of sandlot teams.

"That's when the Braves were in Boston," he says. "One day they had tryouts at City Stadium and I did pretty well." But his parents wouldn't hear of his leaving school to play ball. In the meantime a new sound was beginning to take him away from that of horsehide on leather.

"My friends started turning me on to groups like the Clovers, the Dominoes, and the Spaniels," says Parris. "The songs were easy to sing. I knew the music was kind of sloppy, that it wasn't done well, but there was just something about it that caught my ear, something about those four chords. . . ."

Those four chords would usher in an age of harmony. In almost any ethnic neighborhood in the early fifties, especially in the East, in housing project and candy store and schoolyard, wherever baseball cards were being flipped or traded and pennies pitched, there was that sound—caterwauling in courtyards, cascading down the sides of buildings from the rooftop, sinuously drifting out of open basement windows. It was to be heard on the street corners under lamplight or moonlight, or under boardwalks or elevated train lines in the summer, or inside hallways and under stairwells in the winter—an urban, rattling, reckless sound, blending with the sirens and the traffic. In threes and fours and fives, hardly ever twos, they gathered—minigangs, basketball teams, sidewalk social clubs—their heads close together, hands behind their backs, the odd finger sings bass, to serenade the urban passing throng, city girls, and the very moon of love. Most of these serenades would never be preserved. Most of these singers would never leave the street. But in their dreaming voices, their ceaseless quest for harmony, lay the seeds of the future.

By the time it became obvious that Fred Parris's destiny was to be in rock 'n' roll, in a life if anything even more uncertain than pro baseball, it was too late for his parents to prevent it. He was out of school, of age, about to join the army. He'd already formed a group, the Scarletts, and recorded with a label in New York. "Dear One" and "I've Lost" had made him something of a celebrity in the neighborhood, respected for his vocalizing and writing ability.

"We were probably like the only recording group around," says Parris. "Kids just weren't in the business then. So we were big shots because of that. We were cocky and enjoyed all the glory." Those two records went on to achieve positions on national rhythm and blues charts, which was icing on the cake.

"When I started receiving royalties for what I'd done, which to me was nothing, I said, well there's no sense in me going any further, I might as well do this. I'm getting rich." (His laughter here is grounded in irony.) "Then we got lucky with 'In the Still of the Night,' and it was too late to change my mind."

When the song finally broke from the r&b underground to splash across the pop charts in the autumn of '56, Parris was about as far from the center of that acclaim as you can get—he was a buck private stationed in Japan. In fact, only two of the Five Satins who toured the country in the first rush of the song's success had taken part in the original sessions that produced it in the basement of St. Bernadette's Church in New Haven.

"I assumed I was still part of the group," says Fred, a silent, frustrated partner to all this stateside activity. "One of the guys wrote me a letter asking for material, but they weren't really counting on me being back at all. I didn't send them any, because I felt cheated."

Certainly Armed Forces Radio didn't help ease his long-dis-

tance agony. Introducing his song one Saturday on the popular dance-party program as one of the most requested records
in army history (Fred had been doing a lot of bragging), the
deejay proceeded to play Ella Fitzgerald doing Cole Porter's
"In the Still of the Night," a standard that had nothing to do
with Parris's gem of rhythm and blues. Adding salt to the
wound was a magazine article that subsequently circulated
around the base, detailing the life and times of a group calling
themselves the Five Satins. "I'd told everybody in camp that
I was in the group and then the article comes out and there's
nothing in it about me. The picture that went along with it
really blew a hole in me, because I knew all the guys. I knew
they weren't doing what they were supposed to."

The only thing somewhat alleviating the stress of being so
far from the scene of his success were the weekly letters he received from his manager, Marty Kugell, on the progress of his
baby in the realms of Tin Pan Alley. With sales figures like
150,000, then 200,000 copies bouncing in front of his eyes,
Fred could be forgiven his constant daydreams. "I was counting the money," he recalls. "Boy, you know, I'm going to buy
a house, a Cadillac. And I ended up with nothing."

Actually entitled "I'll Remember (In the Still of the
Night)," in deference to Porter, the song was released on Kugell's own Standord label, which he ran out of his house. At
the time there were as many one-shot labels as one-hit artists—hole-in-the-wall operations as starry-eyed and foot-leath-
er foolish as the hopeful neighborhood groups who came to
audition for them, demos in hand, five-part harmonies at the
ready. A box of gummed labels, a cheap master, and you were
in business, with a legitimate shot at selling a thousand or so
records in New York, Connecticut, and Massachusetts. Kugell
himself had signed up at least a hundred exponents of such local talent in Connecticut alone.

None, however, would achieve the success of the Five Satins, whom Kugell had first come upon in their earlier incarnation as the Scarletts. There wasn't any rock 'n' roll on the
radio to speak of then, only rhythm and blues. Because records

achieved so little airplay, record stores would allow prospective buyers to sample their wares before deciding on a purchase. Many groups inhabited the immediate vicinity of the record store, to provide a little added incentive. Kugell first heard "Dear One" by the Scarletts in an even more intimate way. It was loaned to him by a clothes presser in his father's dry-cleaning establishment; the man's son just happened to be a member of the group. Something of a high school impresario already, Kugell promised him that he'd listen to his son's group the next time they rehearsed.

Since the Scarletts were at that point the property of Uncle Sam, their rehearsals were few, if any. Whenever someone found himself home on leave, there were usually four other local cats to surround him. Groups were fluid, careers nebulous; the sound was all that mattered. At the Scarletts' first paid gig, shortly before their record was released on Bobby Robinson's Red Robin label, they received all of two dollars a man. "Half of which we spent on uniforms that consisted of red ties, because we all had blue suits," Parris recalls. To make a living at this nonsense was unthinkable.

On the occasion Kugell caught up with them, the Scarletts were represented by Fred Parris, in from Philadelphia, where he was stationed, shortly to be bound for Japan. Duly impressed, Kugell set up a recording session for Parris, which occurred on one of the coldest nights of the year, at a VFW hall. None of the backup musicians Kugell had invited down to the session happened to make it, so "All Mine" was done a cappella. Thereafter, with Fred facing imminent embarkation, Kugell sought to get all of his work down on tape. He staged sessions every Sunday at St. Bernadette's Church, accompanied by whoever was around, sober and willing to sit in.

"One of the guys in the Scarletts, Al Denby, was in on those sessions," Fred recalls. "He became one of the Satins. He must have been home on leave. We picked up two other guys from the neighborhood. There were different guys each week. There were really only *four* Satins," says Fred, "but you couldn't call yourself the Four of anything in those days. It was uncool.

You had to be the Five." (Like the Five Keys, the Five Crowns, or the Five Royales.) "So we signed up a piano player when we went on the road."

These frantic sessions resulted in the album *The Five Satins Sing,* which contains just about the sum total of Parris's early work, including the initial single released on the Standord label, the uptempo "The Jones Girl," backed with the slower, more intense ballad, "In the Still of the Night." Eventually, of course, the latter was flipped over, thus allowing "shoo doo't 'n shoo be doo" a permanent place in the lexicon of rock 'n' roll, right up there with "sha-bop sha-bop" (from "I Only Have Eyes for You" by the Flamingos) and "dom-de-dom-dom, de-dang-de-dang-dang, de-ding-de-dong-ding" (from "Blue Moon" by the Marcels), although in fact that particular legendary riff was lifted in its entirety from the middle of an existing r&b hit, "Night Owl" by Tony Allen. But six months after its release, "In the Still of the Night" was virtually dead, achieving airplay only in Springfield, Massachusetts, and Dallas, Texas. Kugell's bills were overdue at the distributor and the presser. So when Al Silver, president of the mighty independent label Herald/Ember, home of the Turbans and the Nutmegs, phoned with an offer to distribute the platter, a deal to split net proceeds fifty-fifty seemed like a two-out homer in the last of the ninth. When the net was finally determined, however, Kugell recalls that his first check from Herald/Ember, representing royalties, amounted to $365.69, paid in full.

Greeted with this paltry sum on his return from Japan, sheepish smiles all around, glad hands transferring the blame like a hot coal, and a group calling themselves the Five Satins headlining at the Apollo Theater in nearby Harlem, Freddy Parris was understandably irate. He felt deceived, denied, gypped. He was unable to trust his manager, his record company, or his friends. The measure of his inner turmoil and paranoia can be seen in the series of apparently contradictory moves he next engaged in. Feeling he deserved the Five Satins name at the very least ("I thought it up. I started the group.

I wrote the song. I sang it."), he nonetheless released his first song after returning home under the name of Fred Parris & the Scarletts. It was the obscure "She's Gone," which went nowhere on Marty Kugell's Klik label. Although Kugell was in the process of suing Al Silver and Herald/Ember Records, Parris signed a new contract with them, and put together his own Satins, a group which included Jim Freeman, who was at the time a part of the same bogus Satins who had sold him out while he was in Japan. (With Parris back in the States, the other Satins rather quickly disbanded.) He then broke off all ties with Kugell; they would not speak to each other for ten years. Meanwhile, he had ballooned to 240 pounds, up from his G.I. weight of 185. Before taking his new Satins on the road, Fred suddenly returned to Japan to marry a Japanese woman. He stayed four months, then brought her back to New Haven. Although the marriage would last fifteen years, according to Fred it was never on solid ground.

"Rather than blame the music or anything, I would blame myself," he says. "I was the one who chose to do this, and I guess I wasn't ready to settle down, make that sacrifice. Unfortunately, I didn't find that out until after I was married."

He must have found supreme respite on the road then, as rough as it was. Away from family and friends, contracts and royalty statements, he fell into the camaraderie of the boys on the bus: Frankie Lymon & the Teenagers, Huey Smith & the Clowns, Hank Ballard & the Midnighters. "It was an entirely different life than what I was used to," he recalls. "It was all sort of off the top of your head. 'Hey, I got you guys a gig.' 'Okay, we'll be there. Maybe we can get an advance on next week's pay. As soon as we get through we can go out, meet some girls, have some fun.' There were always girls who would wait at the stage door for you to come out. They kept up with your career; I think that's all they did. They might hang around with you, even go with you if you were going to California. Then they'd stay out there and latch onto somebody else. It was a very free-living thing. That's all we worried about in those days."

There were the one-nighters and the theater tours. Theater tours were better; they lasted six days, six shows a day starting at noon. The show broke Thursday, then moved to another town along the circuit: the Apollo in Harlem, the Earl in Philadelphia, the Royal in Baltimore, the Howard in Washington. Even in the North the acts would put up at black hotels. "It wouldn't make sense to go ten miles out of your way to stay at a hotel you couldn't afford," Parris explains. "You were only making $750 a week for five guys, and that included room and board. So you ended up staying in one room most of the time. Living conditions left a lot to be desired. Usually you set something up in the neighborhood with a lady in a restaurant, who let you eat on credit until the end of the week. The food was always delicious."

Sets were only about fifteen minutes long, enough time to do your hit, the flip side, and the follow-up. But the groups took pains with their performances. For one thing, they dressed to the hilt, in iridescent suits, white shirts, and shined shoes. "We never had any problems with anyone looking sloppy," Fred notes. Then you had your good dancing groups, like the Cadillacs, the El Dorados, or the Dells. "My group was just adequate. We did what was expected. We never looked at our overall career and said, 'We should do this or that.' "

Neither did most of the acts on the bus. It was impossible to foresee, for instance, that Bo Diddley would still be an attraction twenty years later, or that Chuck Berry would wind up revered. "I don't think Chuck was looked on as such a star in those days," Parris suggests. "He became sort of a cult figure when the Beatles came up. What made him was the white audience, because black people, I've found, don't like oldies. They like things that are happening right now; if it was last week, forget it."

Although the Five Satins continued to release records, eventually leaving Herald/Ember and moving on to Chancellor, Warner Brothers, Roulette, Checker, Atco, and others, it was always "In the Still of the Night" that came to the rescue when times were slow. It made the charts in 1959 and again in 1960, each time reviving the group's fading career. It has since been recorded by many acts, from Dion & the Belmonts to John Sebastian, and occasionally it provides Fred Parris with a surprisingly hefty royalty check, but the bulk of the royalties due him will probably never be seen.

"For me it was always a struggle," he says. "It was never a situation where I was comfortable. We kept on working even when the Beatles came here in 1964, with the whole British invasion. We all learned instruments; I started playing bass. The club owners got a real break when the Beatles came in. They no longer had to hire two groups, a singing group and a band, because everybody began to play their own instruments."

But the arrival of the Beatles signaled the end to rock 'n' roll's age of innocence. The Beatles were sophisticated, hip. They brought with them visions of megabucks. Soon would come the advent of the rock 'n' roll lawyer. Anyway, by the mid-sixties most urban streetcorners were becoming too unsafe for midnight harmonizing. Fledgling rock groups moved indoors, tethered to their amplifiers. Phil Spector showed them the advantages of multitracking in the recording studio. For a time it became a seller's market in the rock 'n' roll business— that is, for all but the original harmony groups who were still out there somewhere looking for that perfect, pure, sweet high note they'd left in a doorway long ago.

Slowly Fred Parris's career dwindled to a part-time job. To put food on the table for his wife and three kids, Parris took a variety of outside positions. He built guns at High Standard. He was a chemical analyst for Olin. He became a sales representative for Roskin Distributors.

"I've had a diversified past," he says. "But if you're just going to say, that's it, I quit, then you're not going to do it anymore. If you want to be in it, you've got to keep doing it. Whenever things were right, I'd go out again." And, for certain, "In the Still of the Night," possibly the number one oldie in New York City, wasn't going to let him fade into the nine-to-fives. When the Five Satins appeared at a revival concert at Madison Square Garden in 1969, the response was overwhelming. Most people assumed they'd been dredged up from the pits.

"One story had it that they found us working a carwash," says Fred. "They tried to make us as low as possible. But I was making a pretty good living at Roskin and just singing on the side. When this came up there was suddenly a demand for us. I was being booked on tours, working almost seven nights a week, going to Philly and Boston and Washington, plus working during the day. I had to quit my job."

Again the song had sealed his fate, but this time the ending was a happy one. "Given our track record, we've played many more places than we should have," says Fred. "I've been to Lake Tahoe and Puerto Rico. A lot of the other guys on the circuit were a little bit jealous. In New York they're still in love with the Satins, the doo-wop sound. But we also genuinely put on a class show. When you've got an hour to do in a club, you can't stand there all night and sing 'In the Still of the Night.' " Even the occasional bus tours are more tolerable. "No one's starving now," says Fred. "We don't all have to sleep in the same room."

It was *the song*, in fact, that got him to the doorstep of the president. The Five Satins, Danny & the Juniors, the Coasters, and Bobby Lewis went on a tour sponsored by Young Republicans for Nixon. They were put up at the best hotels, wined and dined by senators and governors, introduced to Tricia and Julie, given a peek at the Oval Office. "We were supposed to meet President Nixon, but he'd already left for San Clemente," says Fred. "They gave me a box of presidential cufflinks, which I still haven't opened."

One day, circa 1972–73, newly divorced and trying to get back into shape, Parris happened on his one-time friend and manager, Marty Kugell. "It was a matter of running into him on the street, and after this much time we'd forgotten our differences." Through Kugell, Parris immediately reinstated his suit for back royalties against the current owners of the Herald/Ember copyrights (Herald/Ember having gone bankrupt years before). It is a delayed, complicated, and no doubt quixotic quest for justice, still winding on with the outcome possibly years in the future. "I'm certainly not counting on it," says Parris. "I'm hoping someday it'll come through, but I figure I'll just let it alone."

Until two years ago, Fred Parris was still making a nice living with the Five Satins, playing the oldies circuit—a string of small nightclubs, taverns, and high school auditoriums. The circuit caters to the growing number of dedicated, paunchy, pushing-forty nostalgia freaks, who gather to pay homage to the echoes of their good times. But Fred, a student of today's changing music scene, finally tired of such a noncreative, repetitious life. "There was pressure building up," he says of his decision to disband the Satins. "I felt I wasn't doing what I wanted to do musically, and in order to do that I had to stop touring. Audiences see you only as an oldie. They want to see you the way you were. Maybe I'll never make it again, but if I have to stick to oldies, I'd rather go out and dig a ditch."

Recently remarried, down in weight to a svelte 185, Parris finds his later work worlds apart from simple, innocent doowop. He's been putting most of his time into a theatrical concept, musically complex, lyrically grand. Supposedly there's been some interest. A script is being prepared to go along with it. "I've taught myself a lot of new techniques," he says. "Right now I have a little Farfisa organ that I use; I'm hoping to get a bass soon. I use a four-track machine and I do all the harmonies myself, so that if I put a new band together, the parts will be very easy for the singers to learn. They'll all be individualized on tape. That's the way I would have done it then, had the equipment been available. If I'd had these kinds of tools to work with I'm sure we would have done a much better job. I could have put everything on tape exactly as I wanted it. But as it went down, I'd have to tell everybody what I wanted at rehearsals; the guys were local musicians who couldn't pick up too quick, and I would end up saying, 'Ah, okay, what the hell, let it go that way.' "

Local musicians, a disorganized scene, a chaotic career, claims and counterclaims, lost love, lost royalties, and one record after another that was released with hope invariably going straight down the tubes. . . . And now even Fred's centerpiece, "In the Still of the Night," has been suddenly threatened—as have so many early classics—by at least one alleged author. It's no wonder Fred's glad to see that none of his kids have eyes for rock 'n' roll. "My youngest son occasionally likes to play my old stuff. He asks me a lot of questions about it, but I don't think he has any designs on following in my footsteps. I prefer it that way. Performing's a rough life. I like what my kids are doing now, because they're all pretty serious about school."

Fred Parris, in fact, seems to have learned from them. He has plans himself for returning to school, to study the craft of this thing that has been, in good times and bad, his living.

"I should have studied before," he says, "but I never took it seriously. Now it's a necessity. It's too late to start over at anything else." He laughs. "I don't know too many teams that would want me now. Except the Mets. They need me."

THE FIVE SATINS
TOP 40 CHART SINGLES

1956 "I'll Remember
       (In the Still of the Night)"
1957 "To the Aisle"
       (with Bill Baker)

Update: Fred Parris is back on the road, with a group called Fred Parris & In the Still of the Night, still getting mileage with his one claim to fame.

PHIL EVERLY

.■

Speaking in New York City, fingers trembling on his desktop, Archie Bleyer, seventy years old, contemplates at some remove the careers of the two young men out of Nashville whom he signed to his label, Cadence Records, early in 1957. The long drift to obscurity after the peak, the self-destructive episodes of the sixties, the dying fall of the seventies . . . "I think Don has made a couple of albums for Wesley Rose's label in Nashville, Hickory Records. Nothing happened with them. Occasionally he plays on some sessions there, but I hear he's a very embittered young man, which is a shame, because he's a talented guy. So is Phil.

"The main thing that happened with them was the friction between the two of them," Archie goes on. "It was always a question of so many people saying Don was better than Phil. Don came up with this, Don did that. Phil was pushed to the background too much, which wasn't at all the way it should have been. I can remember in the early days thinking if I had to choose between them, I'd choose Phil."

Once married to Archie Bleyer's stepdaughter, Jackie, and recently remarried, Phil Everly makes his home in Los Angeles. His latest album, *Living Alone*, was released in mid-1979 to minimal acclaim. Of his private life in the sixties and seventies, of his and his brother's documented problems with pills, of the celebrated onstage breakup of the act in 1973, he is taciturn, protective. "I'm not interested in discussing that anymore," he remarks tartly. "Use somebody else's account of that." Of his relationship with Don today, he will acknowledge only that "We're in touch like normal brothers. We probably know all there is to know about each other, so there's not too much to talk about. We're into separate things and have been for the last five years, which is fine." Chances of a professional reunion, then, appear slim. You wouldn't believe the offers we've had—bigger than we had at Warner Brothers. But we're not going to do it unless it's something spectacular."

About the pains of coming off the high of pop stardom, Phil is somewhat more illuminating in his response. "Remember when you were twenty and you had all that strength, you were out and about, you had more energy, everything was good? Well, you're talking about a time when life was really good for you, when what looks like the best part of your life—to an outsider, viewing me as an entertainer—is over. But that's not my whole life. As you get older you get more realistic about what life is. There's no point hanging onto yesterday, or an idea or an attitude about any kind of fantastic thing, because today is just as good anyhow. I knew at the time rock 'n' roll wasn't something you could build a life on. But making music is something you can't help but do. You do it and you can't stop yourself, and you'll do it no matter what. I sing almost every day to somebody in this house, showing a song, doing something. And every time I sing, whether the audience is one, or whatever, it's the same thing. But a staged performance, bringing in a band and causing complications; I have no reason to miss that. I don't have any negative feelings. I don't think anybody with any sense would. I understand the business. You can't always be number one." Though glibly tossed, like refrains of a song he's often sung, in solitude these maxims, like his guarded privacy, undoubtedly serve Phil Everly well at age forty—although apparently they've been earned at some expense to his confidence.

As revision upon revision blots the true picture of rock's onset, reputations flutter and dance with the whims of each succeeding generation of critics. The more insecure of rock's progenitors, left with no current record sales to bolster their morale, no definitive tome to propagate their accomplishments, are prone to question their contribution, rock 'n' roll itself—as a whim, a mistake, a fickle act of chance, an illusion as fleeting as youth. Passed and surpassed, lapped and buried, even the certified greats in terms of record sales, mob response, and fan adoration can get to feel betrayed by their legions, deserted by history. Healthy-sounding platitudes notwithstanding, Phil Everly has had to fight down such ghostly doubts. They come flashing to the surface, suddenly provoked by a description of the dynamics of the fifteen-minute set, twelve-act bill, so common in the fifties.

"Even if you're only doing three songs, you'll pace them," he says a bit defensively. "An actor who's on stage for ten to fifteen minutes out of two to three hours . . . does he really have time to get into it? The point is not for the actor to get into it, but for the audience to. It all depends on whether you can stand and deliver. You feel something at one time. You don't feel it on a progressive basis: I'm working up the ability, the emotion to sing this song. You have what you have at the time you're doing it, and it'll be different every time you do it. It's the same thing when you cut a record. It takes six months to do an album now. We were cutting albums in six days—and everybody considered that slow. Like they were being indulgent when we'd only get two sides done in three hours.

"But what's the real question?" he asks brusquely. "Are you comparing people's ability at that time and now? Would the fifties performers be able to go out and do a two-hour concert? It sounds like you're trying to say how unprepared rock 'n' rollers were. They really didn't know what they were doing— which was the thought process that permeated the fifties. You had to fight against it. 'They really don't know what they're doing.' 'This isn't really going to last because they're not really performers.' But you must relate that to this: all the acts that you now see doing two hours are based on those original people. The short shows, the immediate aspects of it, helped create the foundation upon which this new stuff is built.

"In the fifties there were guys doing the same thing," Phil asserts. "They were doing two hours, but not on The Show of Stars, because The Show of Stars had fifteen acts and the whole show was two hours. Everybody only remembers the things in the big cities, but that's only sixty days, and then you'd have the rest of the year to play. You'd be playing a park, you'd be playing by yourself, doing forty-five minutes, an hour. Most of the acts, like Sam Cooke and Jackie Wilson, wanted to do more and more. It wasn't that they weren't capable of performing solo—but to draw people in the promoters wanted ten to fifteen names. Eventually all the acts got wise that they could do it themselves, because all the times they weren't playing for Irvin Feld or Alan Freed they were making more money and drawing more people. If you stayed hot you outgrew big shows. By 1960 they were pretty much gone anyhow."

Phil concedes the betrayal issue as far as airplay, however. "What deserts you," he says emphatically, "is usually the disc jockey. What really happens is that you have people who like to hear you sing, but the only way they know you have a song out is if the disc jockey plays it. If he doesn't play it, they don't know you have it out."

Archie Bleyer, in search of an explanation for the Everlys' relative failure, solo or in tandem, to find much comfort in the realms of country music—as have so many lapsed rock 'n' rollers, from Brenda Lee to Conway Twitty—sees it more two-way. "They did not cultivate the deejays as much as they should have, and that could prevent a record from getting on the country charts," he offers. "A deejay can't make a record, but he can keep it from being made. You've got to have good rapport with the deejays."

Meanwhile, when the hits stopped coming in America, the Everly Brothers found a home on the European and Australian charts, even while the Beatles, on these shores, were being touted as the second coming of the same Everlys, an irony certainly not lost on Phil. "The Beatles were big enough to admit they were influenced by us, and a few other groups have said so, too. Most people who are really aware in the industry know who did what. I know it, but it doesn't do any good to toot your own horn. It's not important anyway."

Beyond taste, beyond changing trends, beyond conviviality with the local spinners, lies politics. Did the fact that the Everlys dropped out of the revered and exclusive Grand Ole Opry turn the Nashville regulars forever against them? "It was a matter of percentage," Phil explains. "We had to pay a percentage of our earnings to them, and we didn't use them. You were supposed to appear there one Saturday out of every four, and sometimes that was impossible." Still, as Archie Bleyer notes, "Most of the country performers arranged their schedules so that they could be back in Nashville for the Grand Ole Opry; it was that important to them."

Or maybe the Everlys' turning point was the shedding of Wesley Rose, one of the founders of the Country Music Association and their original manager and music publisher, moreover the man who introduced them to Felice and Boudleaux Bryant, writers of so many of their early hits. Rose was instrumental in getting them started, keeping them going until they signed on with Cadence, and even then, with Archie, behind every major decision; maybe their rift kindled an undying flame of animosity in the hearts of the anti-rock brigade coursing through the countryside in those grassroots primeval days, still evident now wherever pedal-steel guitars and mandolins make country music. Phil Everly prefers to remain apart from anything too painfully obvious.

"I could relate to you things that happened and speculate on this, that, and the other thing, but it won't do us any good," he reasons aptly. "I have my CMA card, Number 5 or

Number 6. Don and I were and are country at all times, but it seemed we were always carrying a banner, just by the nature of our music, I guess. We were in the forefront of every fight in rock 'n' roll. It was a fight with your own tastes pitted against established trained people. That's what rock 'n' roll was all about.

"The whole world was anti–rock 'n' roll. Nobody in authority knew what was going on." He betrays his vehemence with a chuckle. "The only ones who knew what was happening were the acts. So the tendency was to leave you alone and let you do what you did. Afterwards everybody would explain how you did it. We never paid any attention to what we were doing; we were fairly ignorant of its value and impact, which, I think, is why rock lasted. It's when you begin analyzing rock 'n' roll—which is what the industry started to do, to figure out what was going on, and then to try to create it—that you get into trouble. The smart older people were the ones who would let you do as much as you could and guide you to a point where you were getting as much of yourself out as possible.

"Actually, rock 'n' roll is an asinine phrase. It was coined after the fact. White rock 'n' roll is really a combination of rhythm and blues and country—the new wave of country music. Boudleaux Bryant understood that, because he's a smart man and he didn't have any of the prejudices the rest of them had. Wesley had always considered us country, whatever he meant by that. I've never been one for labels, because obviously Don and I were already strange down there. We had long hair and we looked different. We were the first ones who wore Ivy League clothes on the Grand Ole Opry stage. As silly as it sounds this many years later, I still resent people who are older than me who have long hair, because I remember them on my case."

Nevertheless, in the mid-sixties, the Everlys found themselves effectively shut out of the country market. Wesley Rose, who would control their publishing until 1970, also saw to it that they couldn't record any more songs by the Bryants, whom he had under contract. "It was very difficult for us after we left Wesley," Phil admits. "But then country music itself matured. The young guys who really understood white rock 'n' roll, the young men who came up in the late sixties, brought country music to its place today; not the old people being purists, but the young jocks, the young ears." By now, anyway, it must be water under the Tallahatchie Bridge. "Don and I knew who we were and what we did," Phil explains patiently. "We knew we weren't Roy Acuff. We knew that before we came to Nashville."

Before Nashville the roads were certainly all of the woodsy, leaf-laden country variety, stretching through the South and Midwest. Although Don was born in Brownie, Kentucky, and Phil two years later in Chicago, Illinois, most of their youth was spent in Iowa and Tennessee, singing on the radio with their parents, Ike and Margaret. "In the school we went to in Iowa there were three kids with long hair, Don and I and another kid who was crazy too. We thought we were theatrical. That's why we felt we had to do it. Don had sort of a ducktail. Maybe he read about it in a magazine or somewhere."

But the Everlys were certainly not regarded as celebrities by their schoolmates. "Nobody thought anything positive about what we were doing," Phil remembers. "It was country music, and that's when country music was put down by everybody. Socially it was hillbilly stuff. Everybody was into Eddie Fisher." Meanwhile, live radio was dying; Ike Everly was making plans to become a barber.

In 1955 his two sons migrated to Nashville from their last radio job in Knoxville. "It was the first year anybody had heard of Elvis," says Phil. "The people there knew something was going on with him because he was stealing the show from everyone. He was on the Hank Snow tour, opening the show at first, but finally they had to put him on last, because all the stars were walking off the tour. Everybody with long hair was immediately thought to be in the same area, but the area wasn't big; it was just the one guy, they thought. They didn't know it was going on all over the country."

The two high school bohemians with their ducktails and big-city fashions soon became somewhat shadowy figures haunting the alley of the Ryman Auditorium, where the Grand Ole Opry was held every Friday and Saturday night. They attempted to score contacts and occasionally played one-nighters, where they got paid in apples. "You'd drive hundreds of miles to make ten dollars, and then you'd have to kick back five." They auditioned for every record label in town. "We were too radical, too different. One of them said for us to wait two years until our voices matured." Even Archie Bleyer at Cadence turned them down the first time he heard them.

Half in love with the memory of those frustrated, starving times, Phil enjoys the story of how they made their audition tape for Archie Bleyer—an anecdote, he says, which has since been canonized on celluloid in some obscure rock 'n' roll bio-pic. "We didn't even have enough money to pay for an audition tape. A friend of ours, a girl we'd met in Nashville who used to feed us occasionally, arranged for us to get the tape done with someone she knew. So we made the tape, and after it was too late, after we'd already wasted the time, she explained to him that we didn't have any money. She took care of it in some form or fashion, I guess. But then when we went upstairs to the street, we found that our car had been towed away. It was impounded. So we had to go back downstairs and she had to borrow the money to get our car out of the pound from the same guy we hadn't paid for the tape. It was far-out." That Archie, their future benefactor, turned down the tape only enhances the romance. "I tell you, the period was so exciting and fantastic, when I think about it, talking to you about it makes me look back on it with such relish."

Eventually their genius was recognized . . . by CBS. "We did four sides for them in about twenty minutes. Carl Smith's road band had just driven in nonstop from California and they hadn't even gone home yet. They weren't exactly in the mood to hang out. We'd rehearse a song with them and cut it, rehearse another, cut it." Off that maiden session in a hotel basement came "The Sun Keeps Shining," written by Don. "There was a rumor that they'd released the others after we had 'Bye Bye Love,' but nobody ever heard them. The whole thing was like a shock to us. All the songs were atrocious."

Living on money from home plus the royalties Don had made from the country song he'd written for Kitty Wells, "Thou Shalt Not Steal," Phil and Don were on the brink of abandoning their struggles in Nashville and joining their father in Chicago, where he'd relocated to work the construction trade. Both were high school graduates, Phil getting his diploma through a correspondence course. It was time for such able-bodied young men to help the family. But a man named Dick McAlpine convinced the brothers to linger in Nashville another day, another week, another winter; there was a TV show he was trying to put together. Overnight success was a coaxial cable away.

Several months later, the TV show shot down, the Opry still turning deaf ears, Archie Bleyer came back to town and Wesley Rose finagled another audition for the two young songwriters whose work he'd been so diligently trying to plug. Whether it was their new, improved connections, the spreading country coattails of Elvis, or whether in fact their voices *had* matured in six months, this time Archie sprang for a contract. He also just happened to have a song for them, a Felice and Boudleaux Bryant song, published by Acuff-Rose, entitled "Bye Bye Love." According to legend, the song had already been rejected by some thirty artists, including Gordon Terry, signed to Cadence at the same time as the Everlys, who resisted because he felt Archie Bleyer was forcing it on him. The Everly Brothers had no such complaints. "We'd have sung anything," says Phil, "because we knew you got sixty-four dollars for a recording session. When you're hungry you get to thinking about those things."

Pocketing the sixty-four clams, the Everlys continued their good fortune. "A friend of mine named Pat Kelly had a father who ran a tent show," says Phil. "It was a real carny operation. Occasionally Bill Monroe would come on the tour. A couple of times we rode with him in his limo—thirteen of us.

That's the way they toured in those days, in limos and station wagons. The station wagons were for equipment. Most of the time you rolled at night, what you call 'hit and run.' You'd sleep in the car, or else in a real dive. I mean we hit some really seedy places, places where you wouldn't want to use the toilets. Real skid row. And it was the biggest tour we'd ever been on," he recalls with a smile. "We'd only gotten it because our friend had talked his father into hiring us. We were making ninety dollars a week and thought it was hot stuff."

While the tour wound through Mississippi, Alabama, and Florida, "Bye Bye Love" was released in Nashville. When the Everlys returned home the song was in the country top ten. "I was at my girlfriend's house," says Phil, "and my brother called me and told me Ed Sullivan had called. Just like in the movies. I said, 'Ha ha ha ...' " Immediately the tours improved. Instead of thirteen in a limo, it was two on a bus to Cleveland, where deejay Bill Randle, one of the first to play Elvis, had broken the record wide open in the pop market.

"There was a great division between country and pop in those days," notes Archie Bleyer. "Wesley and I had a big long discussion. He wanted them to be country. I said the public has decided otherwise."

From Cleveland it was on to Buffalo and points nationwide. They bought a car with the advance they got from the publisher, Wesley Rose, who became their manager. "In those days you didn't make much money with a hit; a couple of hundred dollars a night was a big deal." Decidedly better than apples, however. They came off the road and back to Nashville only long enough to pick up some CMA awards, for Don to peek in on his wife, Suzie, for Phil and Don to buy a house for their parents (Phil lived there for a while, across the street from Don), for the Everly Brothers to record a side or two ... or ten. "We did a whole album in a week," marvels Phil. "We were running out of things we knew, so that created a little tension, because it didn't look like we'd be able to complete the album before going back on the road."

Cut over four sessions, "Wake Up Little Suzie" was released

without Archie Bleyer's total approval. When it went to Number 1 he may have been somewhat mollified, but right away the dealers and distributors demanded more product, something to capitalize on the Everlys' growing reputation (which might well evaporate inside a month). So "Should We Tell Him" was released from the album and it bombed. But "All I Have to Do Is Dream," backed with "Claudette," retrieved them from the edge of obscurity, even though there was tiff over that too, with Archie and Wesley each preferring different sides.

Don and Phil were now past the tent-show stage forever, on the open road with tours promoted by Howard Miller in Chicago and Irvin Feld and Alan Freed in New York. "It was more fun to tour than anything," says Phil. "The days were really golden. For three years Don and I kept having hits and getting progressively bigger." Big enough to afford separate rooms. "I could finally quit sleeping with his feet in my face." On the Show of Stars they became fast friends with Buddy Holly & the Crickets. "Jerry Allison was the most creative rock 'n' roll drummer I'd ever seen. He and Buddy were sensational musicians." On the Alan Freed extravaganzas they'd play until four in the morning. "There was always a finale of 'The Saints Go Marching In.' We'd be watching the balcony shake. I thought it was going to come down." Backstage the gaming was as intense as the music. "Some people played cards; we gambled with the band, big dice games where I used to lose my money. Our road manager finally had to give me a budget of twenty dollars a day because I'd lose it all." But, as opposed to many other groups of the time, finances from stage shows and royalties were not a problem. "We had no dishonesty of that sort around us," Phil maintains. "We did real well."

By 1958 they'd graduated to headlining their own tours, attracting their own distinct clientele of groupies. "You didn't call them groupies in those days, they were just fans, without the sexual implications. Once in a while a girl would expose her boobs and ask you to sign them, but that was usually a barmaid or an obvious floosie. Most of the girls were discreet in those days, or pretended to be, though they'd scream and faint and tear at your clothes, unless you told them not to. I remember one girl who always cried when she saw me. One time I had gotten out of a car with Buddy Holly and I was already in the hotel; Eddie Cochran was getting out of the car and I saw the same girl doing her crying act for him. That kind of keeps your head on straight."

So did the media evaluation of rock 'n' roll, circa 1958. "One time a photographer lined us up with the Shepherd Sisters and they took a profile shot of us and a profile of them. The caption was: 'The only way to tell the difference between rock 'n' roll girls and rock 'n' roll boys is that the boys' hair is longer.' That's what it all came down to for them. Everybody in the entire established music industry was continually telling you that rock 'n' roll was going to die out. Every interviewer in 1957–58 asked me what I was going to do when this was over. You get asked that enough and you get to wondering yourself."

Especially when acts on the tour would ride high on the top ten one month, then mysteriously vanish the next, victims of the public's notorious forgetfulness, or victims of their own acclaim: Buddy Holly chartering a plane in a storm so he could get to the next town with some spare time to do his laundry; Eddie Cochran's limo crashing on the way to the airport. "When you saw a guy bite the dust," says Phil, "it was like seeing a buddy shot in the war. You know, you think you're next."

But the only place where the Everly Brothers' number came up was on the charts, six top-ten records in two years. They featured Jerry Allison on the drums in " 'Til I Kissed You." "Let It Be Me" was their first recording date outside of Nashville—in New York City, a town they otherwise had little use for. "New York was a joke to us," Phil says. "It was a joke to all of rock. Buddy Holly, Buddy Knox, Jimmy Bowen, Eddie Cochran, you name them; they were all country, born and bred. Tin Pan Alley was jive and we knew it." Yet as the years went on, these rock 'n' roll primitives veered ever closer to the Tin Pan Alley ideal, most of them releasing their own cover versions of standards as soon as they could, priming the act for Vegas. "There was a period in 1961 or so when it seemed like that's what you should do," says Phil. "They even put Elvis in Vegas." Nearly all of them, even in the midst of the tumult, were asked to be models for "the youth."

"There was a kind of psychological persuasion to induce you to try not to have your picture taken with a cigarette. They approached you as if you had a moral responsibility, the same way they approached baseball players. That was at a time when a baseball player would never do a beer commercial." He snickers like an unregenerate public school scamp. "I've got hundreds of pictures with cigarettes hanging out of my mouth." By the mid-sixties the rock 'n' roll role model would be turned inside out: the cigarettes, reefers, would be prominent in T-shirt pocket, paraphernalia on tabletop, sweet smoke ever present. Phil Everly's trip took place in another era. "We had a band on tour with us once who considered themselves above and beyond rock 'n' roll," he elaborates. "In those days any man who played a horn thought he was a jazz musician, which is a lie. Our band was really rough and rude, and at one point they were busted for grass—which nobody even knew they were using. All during the tour they'd been cutting us down about how seedy we were, and how fantastic and professional they were, and all the time they were space-city!"

The rebuke, even in retrospect, seems genuine. It is no mere camouflage, no smokescreen remnant from the days of repression or false face automatically pulled for the camera. Those floating drug-warped heads of the sixties and seventies are a rock 'n' roll millennium from the world Phil Everly claims to have seen in the late fifties and early sixties.

"Eddie Cochran was a real fun guy," he says, perhaps warming to a lascivious tale. "One time Frankie Lymon, Buddy Holly, Eddie and I were all up in his hotel room, and it was loaded with girls. The police came up with the hotel manager and threw everybody out, and as we were going out the door, the last two out were Eddie and me. And as Eddie went out he told the manager, 'If Eddie Cochran was here he wouldn't let you do that.'"

By the early sixties even the deriding taunts of strangers had dwindled to the passing snide remark. "You'd get into a cab and the driver would say, 'What are you going to do with that *banjo?*' He's talking about your guitar. The word *guitar* was not common until the Beatles came over. They put a class element into rock 'n' roll because they were British. The president's daughters—Johnson's daughters—came to see them. All of a sudden you were in an art form. Crazy, isn't it?"

When the Everly Brothers left Cadence in 1960, it was for a ten-year, one-million-dollar deal with the newly formed Warner Brothers. "It seems small now," Phil ruefully notes, "but it was the biggest contract written at the time." A neat slap at the critics, that. "We probably wouldn't have been so determined to get ourselves a long-term deal if we hadn't been brainwashed with the idea that rock 'n' roll was going to die." So security then, a notion seemingly foreign to these ranks of hell-for-leather, backwater, backbeat ruffians, proved the best reward. Their first release on Warner's, "Cathy's Clown," was their biggest international seller. But for the remainder of their contract they would reach the top ten only five more times, never higher than Number 6, the last time in May 1962, with "That's Old Fashioned," a curious commentary on their faltering position in this soon-to-be-ordained art form. "It doesn't happen to you suddenly. You don't panic inside yourself right away," Phil says of the realization that the hits have stopped coming. "You have to know that every time you put out a record you're shooting dice." But when you're used to the top-five rush, anything less just doesn't provide the same get-off. A few placebos in a row and a sort of withdrawal could set in.

"Being hot on records lasts about five to six years for most acts. It's true of Elton John, it's true of even the Beatles," Phil believes. "Then it peaks out and the next thing comes along. The longer your career lasts, the more you can see a pattern to it. If the work you did in the initial period is good, it will hold. Don and I survived as long as we decided to, and we quit it when we quit."

But maybe to survive in the absence of that rush, an artificial stimulant is needed. Both Don and Phil, according to published reports, were hooked on pills during the early years of the top-five drought. Phil cured himself; Don ultimately attempted suicide. Living in Nashville, Don Everly is unavailable for comment. Phil declined to speak for him, or for himself on the matter. Concerning the reasons behind his decision, perhaps impulsive, to stalk off the stage mid-set at a 1973 concert at Knotts Berry farm in Buena Park, California, Phil replies: "I don't discuss these issues publicly; it's not something I do. It's nobody's business."

Phil survives today at a low-key, shambling, nontaxing pace, collaborating on songs with several people, three to four hours a day, three to four days a week. "If you keep at it steady, you'll eventually turn out a lot of things," he says. Asked what, he revealed a song for an upcoming Clint Eastwood film, another album, and this rather startling disclosure: "I just played in public for the first time in three years, at the Palomino. It's close by, and I didn't have to work too hard. I surprised myself." This with an offhand shrug of self-deprecation, from a man obviously wary of any mention of such things as comebacks. The thought must seem too awesome, or else totally beside the point.

Then again, perhaps Phil Everly sees it as comical, like this story he tells on himself about what might have been a real comeback at the end of the sixties. "It was the stupidest thing I've ever done," he says with a laugh. "Bob Dylan came backstage when Don and I were at the Bitter End in New York, and I asked him if he had any songs. He showed us one, but he sang so soft, swallowing his words, that I couldn't quite glom the lyrics. It sounded to me like he was singing 'Lay lady lay, lay across my big breasts, babe.' So when he got finished I said, 'Bob, I don't think we can get away with that.' And we didn't take the song." Later in the year, of course, Dylan himself brought "Lay Lady Lay" to the top ten, cementing a kind of comeback of his own.

So Phil can only downplay this event in his life, just another gig. Yet in a few minutes his real feelings shine through the mist. "Before that show I just didn't want it bad enough to do something about it," he admits. "But it was fun and I had a good time. I'll do it again, until it doesn't make me feel good anymore."

THE EVERLY BROTHERS
TOP 40 CHART SINGLES

1957	"Bye Bye Love"
1957	"Wake Up Little Suzie"
1958	"This Little Girl of Mine"
1958	"All I Have to Do Is Dream"
1958	"Claudette"
1958	"Bird Dog"
1958	"Devoted to You"
1958	"Problems"
1958	"Love of My Life"
1959	"Take a Message to Mary"
1959	"Poor Jenny"
1959	" 'Til I Kissed You"
1960	"Let It Be Me"
1960	"When Will I Be Loved"
1960	"Like Strangers"
1960	"Cathy's Clown"
1960	"So Sad"
1960	"Lucille"

1961	"Ebony Eyes"
1961	"Walk Right Back"
1961	"Temptation"
1961	"Don't Blame Me"
1962	"Crying in the Rain"
1962	"That's Old Fashioned"
1964	"Gone, Gone, Gone"
1967	"Bowling Green"

Update: No new Phil Everly album has yet been released but the soundtrack album of the Clint Eastwood film *Any Which Way You Can* has a Phil Everly tune on it, "One Too Many Women in Your Life." And Phil has released a single, "Dare to Dream Again." Don Everly has recently surfaced with a band he calls Dead Cowboys. Speaking in *Billboard* magazine last July, he said, "A lot has been put in print that I'm bitter about what happened with the Everly Brothers, and that's not true. It was a period of my life that I'll never forget."

JO-ANN CAMPBELL

．＂

"*Y*ou know the old saying—when you get married it's all over."

The utterer of this timeless bromide is Jo-ann Campbell, otherwise known as the Blonde Bombshell, the reet and petite lady rock 'n' roller who with her outrageous costumes and her majorette moves, was virtually a staple on the Alan Freed stage show and tour from 1957 on. In a melodious drawl redolent of the Jacksonville beaches where she grew up jitterbugging, and seemingly unaffected by the young adult years she spent living with her parents in an apartment in Queens, New York, trying to make it on Broadway, she half-jokingly reflects on the cause of her retirement from rock 'n' roll in the midsixties at the age of thirty, an action that broke the heart of many a perspiring adolescent boy. That she sits in Nashville these days, spoken for, nested, and secure among clippings and posters and photos—an everyday housewife and mother of a teenage son, directing her nervous energies toward her work for the Humane Society and her fifteen dogs and a cat—is one of the tougher truths to grapple with for a legion of Elvis lookalikes in mid-calf chinos and snap-on shoes, those of us who packed the Alan Freed shows to bulging, causing the rafters at the Paramount to shake with our fevered stomping; arriving in the morning to stay all day and weather the inane flicks to watch the show repeat—that is, to watch Jo-ann twist and shout her way through Chuck Berry's "Rock and Roll Music," Bobby Darin's transmogrified "King of the Hop," or her own "Motorcycle Michael." That she is a suburban lady of the manor now, well beyond the enticements of the bandstand, means for sure that rock 'n' roll was always just a momentary dream, a party doll gone forever.

"It was a glamorous time," she reflects. "The performers in those days were really looked up to. Alan had something like a twenty-five-piece orchestra with two drummers for those shows, and when that band kicked off, let me tell you that whole audience came to its feet and cheered. You just can't describe the sound and the feeling and the emotion that came alive in that room." Mere description would not suffice, anyway, especially for those upon whose hearts the Blonde Bombshell is indelibly stamped.

"I've always hated that name," she replies unmercifully, the last of the dream swatted with a careless backhand. "The only reason I didn't argue about it was because Alan gave it to me, and I loved him very much. I thought he was a superman."

Others regarded Freed less adoringly. But Jo-ann believes he was the main reason she began to rock 'n' roll, circa 1956. Before that she was strictly a dancer with eyes for the gypsy life on Broadway. In Jacksonville, where she lived for her first fifteen years, the only child of an automobile salesman, she'd been dancing since the age of four. At Fletcher High she was a drum majorette. "I had done so many things in Jacksonville, but my Mom and Dad realized I wouldn't have the opportunity to go any further unless we moved to New York. I really didn't want to go because I was having a terrific time where I was." Her family, of course, prevailed, and Jo-ann transferred to Bryant High in Queens, New York.

"For a year I really hated everything," she says. "My whole life changed so drastically." She took dancing lessons three days a week—tap, ballet, and acrobatics. Shortly thereafter she dropped out of Bryant to enroll in the more professionally oriented Lodge School. By seventeen she'd been through Germany, Turkey, Greece, and Africa with the USO. "I mostly slept," she recalls. By eighteen she'd played the supper club circuit with Ernie Hayden. But Alan Freed still claimed the largest piece of her heart.

"If I wasn't out dancing somewhere, I was in my bedroom with the door shut, listening to Alan Freed," she says. "When he had a stage show at the Brooklyn Paramount, I went and stood in line with a couple of my friends, and finally we got in." On the bill that day was the lady truckdriver Lilian Briggs, in clinging gold lamé, belting her hit, "I Want You to Be My Baby," and playing the trombone. It seems Jo-ann— good-looking ambitious, pushing twenty, and discouraged by her fruitless Broadway rounds—must have had some kind of revelation in the darkened theater. "I said to myself, this is it, I've got to be a singer, I've got to sing rock 'n' roll, and I've got to be on an Alan Freed show someday."

But aside from Lilian, who was more of a nightclub performer, there were few if any female singers in the rock 'n' roll business of 1956–57. The black women like Ruth Brown and LaVern Baker were really rhythm and blues shouters The white women of the Top 40 like Gogi Grant and Teresa Brewer, or the Sisters McGuire, Andrews, and Fontane, were pop stylists. Some, like Debbie Reynolds and Doris Day, had separate careers in Hollywood. Others, like Patti Page and Jo Stafford, were big-band singers approaching the end of their era. In Nashville, Brenda Lee was only eleven-going-on-twenty-six; Connie Francis was releasing clinkers on MGM; the Shirelles were still the Pequellos, singing in the projects in New Jersey; Connie Stevens was years away from borrowing Kookie's comb.

None of this impeded Jo-ann Campbell; in fact it probably helped. "I always knew if there was a rock 'n' roll show, I was going to do it," she says. It took her just a year to connect with Alan Freed. Along the way she cashed in on her other dream, arriving on Broadway. It was by way of Harlem. "Back in

1956 there weren't any white girls who could work the Apollo Theater and be accepted, and I was," she states proudly of those early rock 'n' roll shows with the Five Satins, the Dells, and Clyde McPhatter. Not that she was planning to move from Bayside. "I never went out of the theater except to eat lunch and rush back. My Mom and Dad would take me there in the morning and pick me up at night."

Her Broadway breakthrough arrived long after she'd given up on ever having her name in those bright lights as a dancer. "It didn't dawn on me until after about a year of auditioning that they were never going to take a person five-feet tall into the chorus line. That's when I said, 'There must be another way.'" The other way was Jocko Henderson's show at the Loew's State, with the Diamonds and Mickey & Sylvia. Immediately thereafter, Alan Freed beckoned. "After I did my first show for him, I worked for him every single show from then on until he left New York."

That so many wholesome youths would erupt in frenzy at Freed's extravaganzas was startling proof, in the music industry's backyard, that rock 'n' roll was a phenomenon to be contended with, not just the ragged front of various fringe groups. Many advocates of morality, decency, and good music united in outraged posses to stem the tide of violence, rebellion, and rampant debauchery this music seemed to propound so loudly. As its symbol and figurehead, Freed was an open and vulnerable target as he roved the countryside in 1958, with his all-star tour in two Greyhound buses.

Along for that fateful ride, Jo-ann Campbell still vividly recalls the dread succession of events which followed one gloomy night in Boston. "We had to stop the show several times for roughhousing in the balcony," she says, "and Alan came out and tried to quiet everybody down. Finally we were able to get it in." After the last of the spectators had emptied into the night, the performers trooped toward the Greyhounds, past the unsettled crowd milling by the stage door. Jo-ann took a seat behind a darkened window. Danny of Danny

& the Juniors went immediately to sleep. The bus slowly rolled out of town, up the turnpike toward Montreal, where, in the morning, the headlines on the newspapers shrieked: Boston Riot: Rock 'n' Roll Show Kills!

"The insinuation of course was that it had happened during the performance, or because of the performance, because of the Alan Freed show itself," Jo-ann says indignantly. "But it really didn't happen at all while we were there. It happened long after we left, on the streets of Boston, around the area, but not during our show, and not because of it. Then the news just spread from city to city. 'Oh dear, there were some people knifed in Boston; the Alan Freed show caused a horrible riot. Cancel them out. Cancel them out.' For the next three weeks we didn't know whether there was going to be a show or not when we got into a town, because the promoters were frantic. Finally the tour had to be canceled with two weeks to go. And that is when Alan Freed started running into all of his problems. He began to get a reputation for having a riot-causing show."

If certain forces within pop music were out to nail Freed, the Boston riot certainly provided the hammer. In 1960 the cross was erected by Representative Oren Harris and his subcommittee investigating payola (pay for play) among disc jockeys. Freed refused to appear before the committee or to sign an affidavit attesting his innocence. As a consequence, he was relieved of his job in New York. "There were so many people, other disc jockeys, who were envious of him," says Jo-ann, "who loved what began to happen to him." Shortly thereafter, Freed was convicted on two counts of commercial bribery by the New York District Attorney's Office, handed a $300 fine, and given a six-month suspended sentence. In 1964, the other shoe dropped when Freed was hauled in for tax evasion and advised to come up with nearly $40,000 in back taxes on unreported income from 1957 to 1959, arguably rock 'n' roll's finest years.

"Everything just piled up on him and hurled him down into

the ground. He literally died of a broken heart. He was quite young and he was stone broke, and that's the way he ended." Out of work in Palm Springs, he died at age forty-three, of uremia, in January 1965. "I felt terrible," says Jo-ann, "because I had no idea he was that sick. As a matter of fact, when he was down and out, I had thought it would be a great idea to call up a load of people and do a benefit for him to raise a bunch of money to help him pay all the taxes he owed. But being young and busy, working at a wonderful career, I guess I didn't settle myself down long enough to realize he was suffering, until it was too late.

"I admire Alan Freed, because of all the disc jockeys—and believe me, all the major ones were taking payola—only Alan told the truth. Some people got out of it very gracefully, although they were just as guilty as Alan. They were able to keep their positions, while Alan Freed lost everything."

Just as that 1958 tour may have signaled the beginning of the end for Alan Freed, for rock 'n' roll it was merely growing pains. The strapping youngster born in 1955 was too big to be brought down with its unfortunate father figure. By the early sixties it had become a commercial giant. On TV, Dick Clark's "American Bandstand" pulled down huge ratings and big bucks. The rock 'n' roll audience not only bought records, but initiated fashion trends and instigated crazes, fads, and fancies, none of them unlucrative to the enterprising entrepreneur. With the influx of Tin Pan Alley veterans and the outflux of some of the original primitives, rock 'n' roll had indeed become as much of an establishment as the pop music it had opposed (and been opposed by) so vehemently.

Not having to depend on hit records to sustain her career (actually Jo-ann Campbell never did have a hit record; her best-known song, "The Girl on Wolverton Mountain," just barely made the Top 40), Jo-ann continued to sing and dance her way across America. "I was able to work anyplace," she says. "I wasn't classified as a girl who only did one thing. Sometimes I couldn't do rock 'n' roll at all. I was booked at the Sands in Las Vegas with Red Skelton, and I had to drop rock 'n' roll

completely. I always did more dancing on stage than singing,
I suppose."

But she was at home in New York too; enough so to become
instrumental in promoting the cause of perhaps the greatest
fad of the era. Fittingly enough, it involved dancing. "The funny thing was," recalls Jo-ann, "I'd originally gone to the Peppermint Lounge to see a friend of mine named Ricky Randle.
He had a band and he was working there along with Joey Dee
and his band. I actually went in there the first time to see
Ricky. But the part that's so pitiful is that Ricky was only
booked there for a week. By the time the place got famous he
was gone. Now I love Joey Dee and I think he had a terrific
group, but Ricky Randle was good too, and he sang real well
and he was very nice looking. He had a nice group too, but
they just weren't in the right place at the right time. In all
truth, if it had not been for Ricky Randle I would never have
gone in there in the first place, and probably the Peppermint
Lounge would never have been heard of." She chuckles.
"That's what you call bad timing."

Nevertheless, Jo-ann and her roommate Loretta (who would
marry and divorce Dick Clark) began to frequent the club on
West Forty-fifth Street, after hours when the music was hot
and the atmosphere was on the close side of intimate. If a
friend was in town, like Tony Orlando or Duane Eddy or Dick
Clark, they'd bring him along. "Before you know it, we were
taking ten and twelve people. We started hanging out there
whenever we weren't on the road." The gossip columns got
wind of the activities at this grungy dive the size of a small
Manhattan studio apartment, with a dance floor in front of the
bandstand and occupancy by more than 127 prohibited by law.
Some photos made the papers, of certain svelte celebrities in
the heated motions of the twist, nudging and bumping up
against mostly unsavory types from the Brooklyn Navy Yard,
who had haunted the place since its pre–salad days. "The
word spread through the neighborhood, and it seemed like in
about two months time you couldn't even get in the place."

The lines formed again; aging Brooklyn Paramount regulars

were joined by those who'd never even seen Jo-ann Campbell wriggle in the flesh. A discotheque craze took over the city, with clubs like Ondine's, Harlow's, the Roundtable, and Trude Heller's doing enormous business catering to the theater people and street people who comingled on those twisting lines. The lines were even said to include Jackie K, the president's wife (who is not to be confused with Jackie *the* K, the deejay Murray the K's wife—who undoubtedly made some of those lines too). Richard Burton's ex-wife Sybil opened a club of her own called Arthur's, to handle the overflow. Joey Dee & the Starlighters went on to a string of twist-inspired hits. The twist begat at least a thousand variations, most of them certified by a Chubby Checker rendition. The true creator of the twist, Hank Ballard, reaped some significant songwriter royalties, and invented a few new steps himself. Even Jo-ann Campbell got a piece of the pie.

It came via the film *Hey, Let's Twist*, in which she starred, along with Teddy Randazzo, who was featured in the role of Joey Dee's brother. "It was not a well-planned film," she offers. "I think we did the whole movie in three weeks. I didn't even know what I was supposed to say until the night before. I'd go home, learn the lines, and run on the next morning. It was not too hot."

Curiously, Jo-ann had much the same approach to record-making. Probably her most successful album, *I'm the Girl on Wolverton Mountain*, was made in less than six hours. "I didn't take making records seriously," she agrees with chagrin, "because I was never out of work. Rather than sitting in New York and dreaming up ways to make good records, I just stayed on the road and worked. I went into the studio once a year and cut a couple of silly records. I wish now that I'd analyzed what I was doing. But I thought 'someday' for the records, right now I'd rather go out and make money and tour the world." Considering the fate of many recording artists of the times, singers whose contracts were shaky and whose royalties were scant, this may not have been such a bad idea after all. "I was so young when I started writing songs," she says, "and I had no earthly idea there was all that money to be made from them. I never got any royalty checks because I never asked for them. I'm not going to say where they went, but I know who's got them." In summing up her Top 40 experience, Jo-ann inadvertently sums up the entire era. "You don't get what's coming to you until you're older and wiser, and you don't get older and wiser until it's too late."

Her recording career does contain some tantalizing near misses, however—even if Jo-ann's own opinion of her work has hardened with the years. "My records were really dumb, high-voiced teenybopper things. I hated them, really. I used to like to sing songs like "Happy Happy Birthday Baby,' slow things, but they never got released because everybody thought of me as a little tiny thing who had to come out there and do something cute. My son, who's fourteen and a half now, used to play my records until I could scream. But he outgrew them about three years ago."

A song she released in 1958, called "You're Driving Me Mad," was her first shot at Top 40 recognition. It epitomized the detours and frustrations that were to trail her and eventually hound her into an early retirement. "All of a sudden, because of a lyric, some stations started banning the record," marvels Jo-ann. The offending phrase, "Drive on baby," may seem tame by today's raunchy standards, or tame even when measured against the standards of rhythm and blues, as written by Hank Ballard and others, but back then, in the nervous atmosphere surrounding the marketing of rock 'n' roll, it must be considered in the context of the sexy Blonde Bombshell who was singing it, already linked in the gossip columns to Bobby Darin and Duane Eddy. The record limped off to oblivion. "It's really funny that that happened to me, of all people," she says, "because I was never one to do anything that was on the dark side."

Her treasured innocence, the deep-seated conservative nature that knelt at the very core of so many gyrating rock 'n' roll pagans, was to spoil her last and best chance for stardom, in 1964. By this time she was married to a musician Troy Seals, and approaching thirty.

"When I met Troy and we fell in love, he was always on the road in one town and I was out somewhere working in another and we didn't get to see each other at all. So we finally decided to get married, put a band together, and travel on the road. That's when I left New York. Sometimes I wish we'd stayed and Troy had toughed it out, but instead we went on the road together for about two years."

As determined as Jo-ann Campbell had been to have a singing career, Jo-ann Campbell Seals was even more determined to have a family. "I wanted to have one child and I had one child," she states. "I wanted to have a boy and I had a boy. All my dreams were fulfilled." In fact, the 1964 single by Jo-ann & Troy on Atlantic Records, "I Found a Love, Oh What a Love," written by but not credited to Jo-ann, was released when she was two months pregnant. "We really should have told the record company, but we didn't think it was going to be a hit. But doggone if it didn't get up on the charts." They were based in Cincinnati, where Troy had some family. The single broke in Atlanta, where the record company summoned them to do a show with Tommy Roe. "By that time I was so big I couldn't have gone anywhere," Jo-ann recalls.

Into the breach stepped Felix DiMasi of Seventh Avenue in New York City, Jo-ann's trusted fashion designer and consultant who had done all her gowns. He constructed her a ruffled pink dress to hide her burgeoning condition. "I still have that crazy dress," says Jo-ann. "We laugh every time we look at it." Jo-ann & Troy appeared in Atlanta, but withdrew from further engagements—including a stint on national TV via "Shindig" and "Hullabaloo." "The minute we told the record company the truth they were really let down," says Jo-ann. "They had big plans for Troy and I. It was just before Sonny & Cher. We were both on the same label. Jo-ann & Troy, Sonny & Cher." She pauses, then shrugs. "It was another situation where it was rotten timing."

For Cinderella midnight was approaching, and the prince was stuck in traffic. After her son was born, she and Troy continued to gig around the Cincinnati area, building up a following and honing a band. Another record, "Same Old Feeling," was released, in the Righteous Brothers' mold. Late in 1965 she appeared for a while on "Where the Action Is," a daytime rock 'n' roll show hosted by Dick Clark. But within six months she and her family were back in Cincinnati, where Troy and Jo-ann played at a club called The Inner Circle. But when James Brown spirited their backup band away with the lure of bigger bucks, Jo-ann decided a vacation was called for. "I really had no idea I was quitting for good," she now says. "But it was the first time in my life that I wasn't working, and I was as happy as I could be. And, as it turned out, I never did go back."

Finally she and Troy gravitated to Nashville, where he works today as a songwriter and a singer, recording for Elektra/Asylum, home of Jerry Lee Lewis and Roy Orbison. But Jo-ann has resolutely avoided a similar return to the spotlight, even though she's been tempted on several occasions. "Whenever I see somebody that I used to work with and they're still in the business, I look up at the TV screen and I kind of say, 'Oh wow, I should be there, too.' But it only lasts for a few minutes and it's over.

"There have been many times when they called from New York to say, 'Get back in here and do some of these shows at Madison Square Garden.' I wanted to so badly, I really did. But I'm also a realistic person. I love the life I have now. I love my family. As bad as I wanted to go back to it one more time, I knew if I couldn't give myself a hundred percent to the business, like I did back in those days, I'd rather not do it at all."

So she makes do instead with her scrapbooks, lovingly compiled over the years, teaming with unretouched photographs and memories, frozen in a time when everyone was limber and whole and excited, flush with hits and hopes, and able to score from first on a single. "Jimmie Rodgers was a superspecial person, probably one of the nicest men I met in the business during that period. Here's a picture of Buddy Holly sleeping on my shoulder. We were both sitting in the same seat on the Greyhound and somebody took our picture. But it doesn't do him justice." She turns another page. "Jackie Wilson was one special guy, a fantastic performer with a beautiful voice, a great dancer."

The photos lie stiff and somber in her lap. Today, Jimmie Rodger walks around with a plate in his head, as a result of a fractured skull. Buddy Holly took a generation down with him in a field in Iowa. Jackie Wilson has been in a coma since an onstage heart attack in 1975. Her old love Bobby Darin, too, is gone. Reduced to a spectator, years removed, Jo-ann has thoughts of visiting New York, perhaps to stage a benefit for Jackie Wilson, like the one she never got to do for Alan Freed. "I wish I knew more about where Jackie is now," she says. "I've heard some things, but I can't get the story straight. I'd really like to contact him, although some people have told me he wouldn't know me." So instead she plans softball games for charity. Like the pictures in her lap, the past seems in so much disarray.

"So many people are just scattered everywhere," Jo-ann Campbell Seals laments. "I've lost track of almost everybody. Duane Eddy called me a few years ago, out of the clear blue sky. I picked up the phone and he said, 'Hi there,' and I knew who it was right off the bat. I think the world of him. He just wanted to check in on me. I have no idea what he's doing now."

JO-ANN CAMPBELL
TOP 40 CHART SINGLES

1962 "I'm the Girl on Wolverton Mountain"

HANK BALLARD

■
■

*H*e was floating in a swimming pool the first time he heard it on the radio, flat on his back in Miami, Florida, in the summer of 1960. "I thought it was me," Hank Ballard recalls. "I was sure it was me. I was wondering why they were playing it on the radio. I didn't find out it wasn't me until a few weeks later." By that time Chubby Checker's version of the song Hank Ballard had written and recorded in 1958 (as the flip side of his hit, "Teardrops on Your Letter"), entitled "The Twist," was on its way to its first appearance in the Number 1 slot on the Top 40 (it would be back again in 1962); Chubby Checker was dancing his way to a career-two-three-four. "They did a pretty good job duplicating my record, man, note for note, gimmick for gimmick, phrase for phrase. Dick Clark auditioned about twenty people before he picked Chubby Checker. And I could have sworn it was me; that's how close he came to my sound."

In 1958 Hank had tried to convince Syd Nathan, then president of his label, King Records, that "The Twist" indeed had hit potential. But with the ballad side, written by Henry Glover, vice-president of the label, heading for the top of the rhythm and blues chart, it wasn't difficult to fathom the reasoning behind King's reluctance to jump on it. "The members of my group, the Midnighters, were doing the dance," Hank says. "They were twisting, so that's where I got the idea of writing the song. But the company thought it was just another record." A couple of years later, however, Dick Clark, the man who'd persuaded Danny & the Juniors to rewrite their "Do the Bop" (turning it into the future standard "At the Hop"), once again heard intimations of immortality on a piece of dented plastic. Thereafter he programed Chubby's version of "The Twist" relentlessly on his "American Bandstand" program.

"I can't complain," says Hank, magnanimous in retrospect. "It's one of the best copyrights I have. Dick Clark did me a favor; otherwise the song would never have been heard. I made a lot of money on that song. Of course it was just a drop in the bucket compared to what Chubby made." In fact, the sudden renewed prominence of the aging flip side did much to fan the brushfires of resentment among the members of his group, the original inspiration for the lyric. Their manager at the time, Connie Dinkler, was convinced that Hank had been ripped off. "She spent so much money trying to overshadow Chubby Checker," Hank recalls with a rueful laugh. "She'd tell photographers to keep the cameras on me. Oh boy, what'd she say that shit for? There was a lot of dissension in the group about that, a lot of jealousy. But even she couldn't get around Dick Clark. He was too powerful. He was like a teenage god."

Meanwhile, Clark was playing Ballard's "Finger Poppin' Time," essentially a remake of "The Twist," which became a top-ten item, reviving his flagging career. "A lot of people don't realize that when 'The Twist' broke for Chubby Checker, we got hot too. We were working 365 days a year. We had to beg for time off." After 1965 Hank Ballard would have all the time off he wanted to contemplate dance steps he might have championed. By then his original group would be long gone too.

"What happened is that they all became Muslims and their whole attitude changed about the music. They didn't want to work any more white dates; they didn't want to sign a white autograph. They became fanatical and I couldn't deal with them." Hank won the Midnighters name in court. He picked up a Cincinnati group that had his old act down cold, and what remained of the beat went on without his original sidemen. "I was mentally prepared for the decline," he says. "You have to save your mind. If you start thinking you're a god up there, you're in trouble. I'm not just into money. I get a lot of spiritual enjoyment out of my profession."

Back in Miami now, where he wrote "The Twist" in 1958, and where he returned for a weekend in 1979 and decided to stay, ensconsed in none of the trappings of royalty (or even royalty deposed), Hank and his second wife occupy a small apartment in a sun-bleached armada of buildings off Biscayne Boulevard, probably not dissimilar to apartments he's lived in for most of his life in New York City, Atlanta, Nashville, and Detroit. Born in Detroit in 1936, he moved to a small town outside of Birmingham, Alabama, with his brother when he was seven years old to live with an aunt and uncle, after his father, a truckdriver, died.

"But I was a runaway at fourteen, man," he exclaims across a dining room table, color TV providing the background music. "That part of the family was heavy into religion. They used to beat me if they caught me humming the blues in the house. They couldn't understand. I was not allowed to sing anything but gospel. I had to get out of that." After the eighth grade he dropped out of school and returned to Detroit to live with another set of relatives. "I was never really family oriented," says Hank. "I have about ten thousand relatives, but I live more like a drifter." Alabama wasn't a total loss, however. "I got my gospel roots there," Hank affirms.

Detroit in the early fifties was quite a funky town. You had the Four Tops imitating the Four Freshmen backing crooner Billy Eckstine. Berry Gordy was still on the assembly line, heading toward a career in the ring. He used to spar with Hank's brother. When Berry began to exhibit other career leanings, a Ballard first cousin, Florence, was part and parcel of his success, putting Motown on the musical map as a member of the *quartet* called the Supremes. (The fourth girl, Barbara, would drop out before the hits started to happen, to become a nurse; Florence would leave in 1967, at a dizzying plateau of stardom, and die tragically, on welfare, years later, while lady Diana sang the blues on the silver screen.) Berry also signed the Four Tops to his fledgling label.

"Berry Gordy made rock singers out of them," Hank Ballard recalls. "I couldn't believe it was the Four Tops when I first heard them. I didn't think they could holler that loud."

At sixteen, courtesy of the Korean War, Hank was allowed to sign on with Ford Motors. There his singing aspirations were recognized by a fellow worker, who was part of a group called the Royals, one of whose members had just been taken into that distant fray. (Hank himself would visit Korea on an Uncle Sam charter, spending nine months there in peacetime service.) The Royals already had an r&b hit, "Every Beat of My Heart," written by Johnny Otis (later revived by the Pips, and then by Gladys Knight and—her cousins—the Pips). Hank, with no professional experience at all to that point, but plenty of amateur acclaim, auditioned, then won a place in the group. He appeared at the same Fox Theater in Detroit where his idol, Clyde McPhatter, was headlining with Billy Ward & the Dominoes. Soon Hank became lead singer and main songwriter for the group. "They were into a real sweet Sonny Til & the Orioles style," he says of the incipient Midnighters. "I had them change to a more driving, up-tempo thing. You know, let's get funky!"

Funky they got; so funky that their records, like "Get It," "Sexy Ways," and "Work with Me Annie," were banned from the radio. They were even arrested for giving lewd performances on stage. "The South was our territory. We didn't do too much touring in the East. They were afraid of our act. Like the Apollo, they threw us out of the Apollo," he says, not bothering to repress the laughter. "We went to Phildelphia, we sold out for the whole ten days. The Apollo wouldn't let us do our act; now you can do anything. They let Richard Pryor come in there and do his act." But what, precisely, did the act consist of? "Doing dirty shit on stage," says Hank nostalgically, "like dropping your pants. I didn't do none of it," he claims, "it was just the group. We had so much negative publicity, then we see Sam & Dave on TV, Frank Sinatra, dropping their pants. . . ." While this story would seem necessarily to be somewhat apocryphal, their racy reputation decidedly was not. "We were a very glamorous group, but mentally I didn't get into it. I'm very low-key. I don't care for all that glamour. It never does anything for me. I call it 'commercial admiration.' But as far back as I remember we had a white audience, because they loved those dirty records, man. We sold a lot of damn records. We used to play colleges. They'd yell, 'Get dirty!' " In his spirited recollection the cry sounds like a killer hook in some avant-garde disco cut. "Most of the stuff that Alice Cooper did, all that stage shit, we were doing that years ago. They weren't as liberal then about a lot of things. They're even cursing on records now."

In those days most of Hank's cursing was done in private, and mostly at his own expense. Foreshadowing the events of 1958–60, Hank undoubtedly cursed his rotten luck when his group, the Royals, became confused with another r&b group, the Five Royales. As Chubby Checker was to succeed them in another decade, the Five Royales wound up capitalizing on a Hank Ballard song much more than Hank and his group ever did. Riding on their hit called "Baby Don't Do It," the Five Royales were inadvertently considered the group responsible for "Annie Had a Baby," well on its way to becoming a huge record. Although the Royals quickly changed their name to the Midnighters, the damage had been done. "The Royales had gone out on tour and really cleaned up. So the promoters didn't want to book us. We sounded similar, you know? The promoters didn't want to gamble on us, even though we were the originators."

The copyright, however, was Hank's, as was one-third of

the proceeds on "Dance with Me, Henry" (probably Henry Glover, vice-president of King Records), on which Georgia Gibbs scored with the mass-market listening audience. It was the answer song, edited edition, expletives deleted, of "Work with Me Annie," itself descended from Etta James's "The Wallflower," which contained the phrase, "Roll with me Henry," deemed too salacious for tender ears. ("Work with Me Annie" was based on a real Ballard ex-girlfriend Annie, who really did have a baby, as per yet another follow-up record, "Annie Had a Baby," written by Henry Glover; "Annie's Aunt Fanny," written by Ballard, closed the series and the soap opera.)

Songwriting has been good to Hank Ballard, but not as good as it could have been had he, like most modern self-contained singer/songwriter acts, insisted on maintaining a piece of the publishing rights. "The company I was with said there's no such thing," he laughs today. "King Records, shit, if you asked for publishing rights, they'd give you your contract back. I didn't know there was so much money involved in publishing. They would tell me, 'You've got to write a hundred songs before you can even get a BMI contract,' and I found out later all you had to do is write one song. On my early tunes I didn't even have a BMI contract. I got it later, but they didn't even tell me I had to apply for it."

Most fledgling performers knew nothing at all about management either. "Man, I hate to even think about the way we were took. But what can you do, man? We were ignorant, and they were the beneficiaries of that. Very few people were lucky enough to find a manager like Elvis Presley had." Hank Ballard & the Midnighters were managed briefly by Jim Evans, who managed Wilson Pickett, among others. "Jim Evans came out to Detroit from New York," Hank notes, "and he tied us up in a contract where he was getting fifty percent of our money. We didn't know a goddamned thing about it. When we found out we took him to court and got out of that contract, man. Jim Evans had about ten thousand acts then; he had everybody."

In those days, the manager's job seemed more secretarial than anything else. If the caller on the other end of the line was willing to pay the price, the manager would accept the date, take his cut, and let the chips fall where they might. Such niceties as career-planning and longevity, routing, and proper accommodations were unheard of. Besides, what did it matter if the next gig was five hundred or seven hundred miles away? Chances are the few black hotels in the vicinity would be filled with truckdrivers, salesmen, or maybe a semipro ball team, anyway. Thus were the acts encouraged to spend their nights on the road. This attitude toward black performers prevailed until Berry Gordy, at Motown, put some structure and guidance into the business and made the artists feel a bit more secure, esteemed as human beings with a lifespan of more than six months to a year.

"They had these houses where you could go to where people would put you up for the night," Hank Ballard recalls, leading into a particularly gruesome flashback, an episode illustrating the awful necessity in those days of having to cover so much ground so quickly between jobs. "I was with Jesse Belvin the day he got killed. About an hour prior to him having that accident, I had gotten out of his car because I didn't like his driver. He was passing on hills and curves, going a hundred miles an hour. Next thing I knew they had a head-on collision. His wife could have lived, but she didn't want to live after losing him. The guy in the backseat, one of the Moonglows, was the only survivor, but he wound up getting hooked on painkillers at the hospital, on morphine, and he had an overdose at a hotel in Harlem soon after."

Such things as cover records, phony contracts, and misdirected royalties momentarily pale. Memory drifts to the good times at the beginning, tours through the Midwest with Alan Freed, then only a small-fry promoter starting to get hot. Six dates with Chuck Willis in Cleveland, Akron, Youngstown, and Cincinnati were the first professional gigs for Hank and the group. "Alan Freed broke things wide open when he started packaging a lot of acts and taking them into ball stadiums.

They didn't have promoters like that before him. It was a big high for me, being independent. I liked being self-employed, yeah. But when I first went on the road, I didn't like it. I was almost tempted to go back to Ford Motors. You could see it was an abnormal way to live. Then it became normal."

Eventually, though, thoughts return to the same bottom line. "What I'm doing now is what I should have been doing then, you know? I should have had my own production company and everything. But we didn't know anything, and there was nobody that was ever going to tell you about it, because you had some dues you had to pay. But I don't hold anybody responsible for my being ripped off but myself. I just read in the paper the other day where Bo Diddley said he sold all his copyrights. Otis Blackwell sold the copyright on 'Fever' to Henry Glover for fifty dollars. Glover also bought 'Dedicated to the One I Love' from Lowman Pauling of the Five Royales for two or three hundred dollars. I can understand the circumstances. Circumstances can make you do a lot of things. I once bought a hit for twenty-five dollars." He chuckles, working his way back to the famous high, satisfied laugh. "I bought it from some guy who was locked out of his hotel in New York. It was 'Switch-a-Roo,' I think. I only gave the guy twenty-five dollars. It did almost half a million records."

According to a certain, possibly marginal, reference source, the writers of "Fever" are listed on the version recorded by Peggy Lee as Davenport & Cooley; years later when the Mc-Coys revived it, Cooley had been mysteriously dropped from the credits, though the publishing company remained Lois. There is no record of who got credit for the original put out by Little Willie John in 1956. Lowman Pauling, along with Ralph Bass, is listed under the Shirelles' remake of the Royales' "Dedicated to the One I Love," but when the Mamas and Papas put it out in 1967, the name Ruff was inexplicably added, and the publishing company had changed from Armo to Trousdale. Go sort it out. You run into a maze of Chinese boxes, doors opening onto empty hallways, laundered signatures, and floating bank accounts. And you can't ask Lowman Pauling anymore; he's been dead five years.

In time you could wind up like Bo Diddley, encountered at a hotel room in New York, staring fixedly at a succession of color TV game shows while outlining his elaborate systems for the eventual recovery of his vanished money. "I don't think the public likes that I was ripped off," he muttered bitterly, proceeding to reveal how the club owners, managers, publishers, record companies, and booking agents of America were having at him still. "I just want to get what I deserve from my product. Just give me mine and I'll be happy."

To which, months later, in Miami, Hank Ballard would reply: "The way I figure it, you're responsible for your own ass."

When King Records was sold to Fort Knox Music in 1967, after Syd Nathan died, Hank Ballard was set free. "The company just wasn't up to par with promotion—they had very poor promotion. But it was one of those things where I had been with them so long I felt like it was family. I had a good rapport going with them and I was afraid to make another move. We always had plenty of work, even when we didn't have a record out. We were red hot for a good ten to twelve years." Of course life with King, as with all families, was sometimes less than sweet. "Syd Nathan was the stingiest man in the world," Hank cackles, lovingly caustic. "Nobody could get as much out of one dollar as Syd Nathan could. Just to prove a point once he said, I'm going to show you how I can conserve $20,000 a month. So he started cutting back on everything, even the electricity. You'd go in the toilet and there weren't no light on!"

Yet Hank's career after King's demise reads like a litany of near misses, botched chances, and strikeouts with the bases loaded. He went in with James Brown, for whom he'd originally helped get a contract at King. "I wanted to be with Polydor so bad," Hank says, "and I figured if I got with James Brown's production company, that would be like a stepping stone. I was with James for a year and a half, but he killed it off. He stopped a hit record on me. That's what fouled it up. I had a record going so hot called 'In the Love Side,' on Polydor. All of a sudden we had 250,000 records gone. I did 'Soultrain' and sales started coming; James got so paranoid and nervous because he didn't have anything going at the time that he called every jock in the country and told them to take it off their lists. I told him, 'That's it for me.' I just walked away from it." Next Hank moved to Nashville and did some work for Shelby Singleton.

"I'd grown up listening to country music—Marty Robbins, Hank Williams. I always did want to get country into r&b. The Commodores, that's the groove I was trying to get into. I did a tune for SS records by Kris Kristofferson, 'Sunday Morning Coming Down.' Now that was a masterpiece, man. I know it because Jerry Wexler heard it and tried to buy the master from them. The record was never released. SS Records was in trouble with the Mafia at the time. Shelby Singleton had to go into hiding for a year, man; they were after him. I did an r&b version of the song that was really pretty. I have a copy of it and I'm going to record it over."

By 1980 the downslide seems to have extended far longer than the upslide ever did. But Hank regards it with remarkable perspective. "You have to condition yourself for the decline," he says. "I've never had a star complex. You can get yourself in trouble with a star complex, thinking you're god. How the hell are you going to be a god when you got a Top 100 out there? Everybody with a hit record thinks they're a god overnight; you got a hundred gods! I've never tried to rise above ordinary people. I like ordinary people. I've never been on that star trip, but I've seen a lot of my associates destroy themselves. Take Clyde McPhatter. He was my idol; I was crazy about Clyde McPhatter. But he had an emotional problem that he never did outlive. He drank himself to death. Little Willie John, the same thing."

Which doesn't mean Hank Ballard has given up on the thought of making music. In April 1979, for instance, he broke a four-year performing fast to headline several nights at the

Howard Theater in Washington, D.C., along with the Flamingos and Baby Washington. "I was scared," he admits. And
shocked by the turnout, a full house each night, complete with
ovations. "I had a hang-up about working in oldie shows. I
just didn't want to get into that oldie thing; I wanted to play
contemporary, you know?"

The success of the show has given him the incentive to think
about a return engagement somewhere down the road, hopefully on the heels of a smash. "I want to concentrate now on
having a big hit record," he says. "I'm going to do what Neil
Sedaka did, come back with a big record, come back with a
hit, man." Toward that end he closed up shop in New York
City, after eight largely fruitless years there, and headed out
where the weather suited his casual clothes. In Miami his pros-
pects immediately improved when he ran into another legend
from the seminal rock 'n' roll days of the fifties, Luther Dixon,
arranger and producer of many of the Shirelles' classics, just
back from an extended sabbatical in Jamaica.

"I had a studio started when I met Luther here," Hank says,
"but I was running kind of short of funds and I needed some
extra money, so I brought him in. He had a lot of contacts
over at Criteria Studios in Miami, and we decided to form a
joint venture. Luther has a monster catalog, about five hundred to six hundred songs. I have close to two hundred. You
can survive as long as you're writing. If a hit don't happen I'll
just keep writing." Their production company's first effort was
Hank's "Boom Boom," released a little late for the disco derby. "We got good reaction on 'Boom Boom,'" says Hank,
chuckling. "A lot of people in Europe had thought I was
dead." Now they're producing Chuck Jackson on a song written by Bob Marley.

"Chuck's been down here rehearsing. We think we can get
a hit on Chuck. Everybody else is coming back. Dionne Warwick is back with a hit. But it's a more competitive scene today," he acknowledges. "Most of the time in the past you
could just walk up to a microphone and start singing any
damn thing. I know James used to do that a lot, and Jimmy

Reed. You have to be more meticulous now. The public ain't buying unless it's good. They want a good track and good lyrics. At one time you could get away with just a good track. You got to have both now. Disco is damn near completely out. The beat is still there, but the lyrics are different. Rock 'n' roll is coming back, same as it was twenty to twenty-five years ago. On the radio it sounds like fifties music."

While most of this new rock 'n' roll is being played by kids who weren't even born when Hank Ballard was out there— getting banned from the airwaves and public stages for being lewd and crude, blazing off-color trails with "Sexy Ways" and "Annie Had a Baby"—some, you can be sure, is the fevered product of ageless vets closer to forty-five than sixteen. And like this latest swing back to rock 'n' roll seems to prove, they were never gone at all, only waiting, enduring, on the outskirts of major cities, at the edges of subsistence. "You know," says Hank Ballard, always ready to see the bright side, "they made a survey and found out that seventy percent of all records are now sexually oriented. If you listen you'll hear sex in nearly every damn thing. Even Helen Reddy had a song out—'Make Love to Me.' Boy," he laughs his swooping laugh, "that was hot stuff."

HANK BALLARD & THE MIDNIGHTERS
TOP 40 CHART SINGLES

1960   "Finger Poppin' Time"
1960   "The Twist"
1960   "Let's Go, Let's Go, Let's Go"
1961   "The Hoochi Coochi Coo"
1961   "Let's Go Again"
1961   "The Continental Walk"
1961   "The Switch-a-Roo"

THE SHIRELLES

SHIRLEY ALSTON

.▪

*W*hen the Chantels went on tour in 1958, their manager Richard Barrett used to sleep outside their hotel room door to prevent any admirers from stealing into their suite in the night to partake of the charms of his favorite girl group. Luther Dixon had a favorite girl group at that time, too, but he wasn't nearly as paranoid. "Nobody could hit on the Shirelles," a friend of his assured. "They were so decent on the road, especially Shirley. Everybody used to be after her, but they couldn't get to her."

No one could touch the Shirelles, not the Chantels, whom they patterned their name after, nor any of the other girl groups of the era. They had class, they had sass, they had panache, but more important, they had Luther Dixon, who made sure they had *hits.* In 1961 they were the first all-girl group to make the top of the charts since the McGuire Sisters in 1958, and the first black girl group, period. Eventually the Marvelettes, the Crystals, and the Chiffons would come, but the Shirelles had it all over those latecomers—two Number 1 songs, six songs in the top ten, and twelve songs in the Top 40, out of twenty-three records on the charts. To find a statistically comparable contender, you'd have to go back to those same McGuire Sisters. The McGuire Sisters, you'd have to say, were the Shirelles of their time, with two Number 1 singles,

five in the top ten, and twelve in the Top 40, out of twenty-
one chart recordings released from 1955 to 1958. (The
McGuire Sisters had eight songs that made the top twenty-
five, and the Shirelles had nine.) So, to finish them off as far
as your all-time girl group, you'd have to wait for the Supremes to get going in 1964–65, with their five (five!) Number
1 singles in a row (they wound up with twelve in all). By then,
however, the Shirelles had done most of the tough legwork. By
then the era would over and the Beatles would be casting the
long shadow of media attention over everyone. By then it
would be like you were playing in a brand-new ballgame, on
Astro-turf.

When the era ended for the Shirelles, it ended with a vengeance. From mid-1963 on, their last seven records (at least)
failed to make the Top 40. Luther Dixon, their beloved producer and mentor, also part owner of their record label, Scepter, departed, having given them his best. Very shortly they
would enter into a lawsuit against the people they'd once considered family.

"During the proceedings I found out things that tore me
apart," says Shirley Alston. "Things I was innocent of. We
didn't know we were being treated this way by the people
there, because we loved everyone. Our feelings were sincere
and theirs evidently weren't. We took to our manager, Florence Greenburg, like a mother. She gave us that mother rou-
tine, and being kids, we fell for it completely. We never
questioned anything she did, not one thing." Once Florence
advised the Shirelles against recording the song "He's a Rebel," claiming they'd get in trouble with it if they tried to sing
it in the South. So they passed it on to the Crystals, who didn't
have any trouble at all in making it a Number 1 song. Something like that was small potatoes, though; it could be laughed
away.

"They supposedly had a trust fund set up for us," says Shirley, not laughing. "But when we got to be twenty-one, there
was no money for us. We never saw it like they said we would.
They should have invested the money for us properly. Being

the top female group in the country, we should have made a lot of money, and we didn't. But we were too busy working and traveling to complain. Nobody was aware of the business. We never gave it a lot of thought. We were young; it was a whole new thing—the glitter of show business. We weren't worried about how long it would last, if things would change the next day. It was a whirlwind thing. It just grew and grew and we couldn't believe all the hit records ourselves.

"The people in the company did well as far as handling our records," she concedes, "but our management wasn't good at all insofar as making us a lot of money. I should have been wealthy and I wasn't. I'm still not. They should have gotten us a super act going. We should have played Vegas, the best clubs in the country. But nobody was concerned with anything except the money that they could put in their pockets. That's what really bugs me to death. If we'd been prepared the right way years ago, right now I could be in Las Vegas six months out of the year, and relax six months a year, or not work at all. If they'd have geared us properly, this is the position I'd be in right now."

The position Shirley Alston is in right now is rather a cramped one, leaning forward on an ancient overstuffed three-and-a-half-legged armchair, of the sort generally found in the decrepit lobbies of hotels named Hotel. Tonight it is in the decrepit dressing room of a nightclub that might as well be named Nightclub, where Shirley, now a solo with a supporting cast of lithe and youthful backup girls, recalling the Shirelles of twenty years ago, is picking up her career again, just where she dropped it several years ago when she left the Shirelles to have another baby, a second daughter.

"When I got pregnant again in 1976, I decided to take some months off," she explains. "After my daughter was born I went back for a few months, but then I called it a day because I was missing her and I stopped for a short time. With my first daughter, who's now sixteen, I was gone all the time. When she took her first steps I was in Germany and I had to see it on film. I didn't want the same thing to happen again. Being

This page
Above left: Fred Parris (bottom) and the Five Satins in the early sixties; *above:* in the early seventies (Parris in the middle); *left:* and in the late seventies.

Opposite page
Top row: Don and Phil Everly on stage at the Paramount Theater, and Phil Everly today (photo: Ethan Russell). *Middle row:* Jo-ann Campbell in 1963 (photo: Michael Levin), and in 1980 with Peanut. *Bottom row:* An early album by Hank Ballard and the Midnighters, and Hank Ballard today.

ROCKIN' AROUND THE CHRISTMAS TREE

By JOHNNY MARKS

PRICE
60c

RECORDED BY BRENDA LEE DECCA RECORDS

...HOLAS MUSIC INC.
... New York, N. Y.

We are The Imperials featuring Little Anthony

STEREO

Opposite page
Top row: Shirley Alston (fore-
ground) with the Shirelles,
and Shirley Alston today.
Middle row: Dave Guard (center)
with the Kingston Trio, and
today (photo: Carolyn Caddes).
Bottom row: Neil Sedaka, in the
early sixties and today.

This page
Above: An early Brenda Lee song;
above right: Brenda Lee today.
Center right: The Imperials, featuring
Little Anthony; *bottom right:*
Anthony Gourdine today.

at home felt fabulous. I enjoyed myself. I shopped, I went on vacations. As a matter of fact, right after I had her, I went out to see the Shirelles performing on a Dick Clark tour. I was in the audience and it felt great. I even did a few shows with them during that year, filling in if one of the other girls was sick.

"But I like my schedule the way it is now. With the Shirelles I was the lead singer, and if I didn't work, they didn't work. Now I'm not obligated to anyone but myself. I'm responsible to my band, true, but they can always work on the side." In addition to her backup singers, Shirley's band contains the usual assortment of strings, horns, and percussion in the hands of the usual gutty, tuxedoed, starving journeymen whose numbers make up easily ninety percent of all such dreamers who ply the trade by night and haunt the Local 802 offices (the musician's union) by day.

While Shirley speaks, her practicing sax man does his best to drown out her soft-spoken words. In an earlier band, in better days, Joey Dee was on the sax. This present sax man is cut from a different reed. But Shirley doesn't seem to notice. "As far as I'm concerned the business hasn't changed at all," she says. "The crowds aren't that much different either. In the early days I toured with the big packages—Lloyd Price, Dick Clark. Today I'm doing the exact same thing with Richard Nader. So it's not very different workwise. But there's a whole new breed of performers. When we'd go out on a bus with Dick Clark, everybody looked out for the other person. We've done tours where if we went into a town and they said to the black acts, 'You can't stay at this hotel,' the white acts would say, 'Then we're not staying either.' As tired as we were from working, we'd drive to another place that would accept us. It was just beautiful."

Sometimes, though, the dives were so raunchy that all the girls huddled together in the same room, probably wishing there was someone like Richard Barrett along to guard the door. "But the arenas were always packed," Shirley notes, "and everybody was hot on the charts, and usually we stayed at very nice places."

Upstairs, late in 1979, the nightclub isn't quite nice, isn't quite packed. But Shirley is polished enough to ignore such things as she showcases for the mumbling audience several of the contemporary tunes she is hoping will launch her latest attempted comeback. "It's very difficult for a person who was popular back in the sixties to have a hit record today," she'd said earlier. "If it happens you better consider yourself very fortunate. I just recorded two sides. I think they're both good. They're not like the old stuff. I tried going in to record companies with the old stuff, but they wouldn't accept it. They wouldn't accept new things from the Shirelles either, because they said they loved the old things. 'I like your new things, but I'd rather play your old things.' And then if you try to record in the oldie vein, you're out of date to them. They say, 'Here you come again with those doo-wop tunes; I can't believe it.' Right now I'm peddling the single, but I don't want to drop it here or there. I want to put it someplace where they're going to do something with it. I don't want it sitting on the shelf. I have a whole album with the Shirelles in the can at RCA." And two solo albums, currently out of print on the now defunct Strawberry Records.

But despite these problems, the kind she's had to deal with since the hot streak ended in the mid-sixties, Shirley remains optimistic. At least she's working. "Though I'm not with the Shirelles anymore," she says, "they work and I work on the strength of our recordings. Once you've had a smash, standard-type song, you can always work, just doing your hits. Even these days when I'm playing a high school, sometimes I may fumble the lyrics, but the kids know them. They learned them from their brothers and sisters."

Tonight Shirley will remember all the lyrics, unaided by the audience, which is of the generation that would have experienced them the first time around—at sock hop and soda shop, pizza parlor, backseat, and basement. Wrapped as they are in a hasty medley, disguised though they may be in a disco beat, the nostalgia beams through. Illuminations of an adolescence spent waiting for that slow dance the Shirelles inevitably provided pierce the whiskey talk and cigar coughing. "Dedicated to the One I Love," "Baby It's You," "Soldier Boy," "Tonight's the Night," "Foolish Little Girl," and especially "Will You Love Me Tomorrow," succeed in silencing the room.

"When I first heard 'Will You Love Me Tomorrow,' I thought it was awful," Shirley later reveals. "As a matter of fact, I started to cry. I said I wasn't going to do it. The demo was just Carole King banging away on her piano. I thought it was a country song. I said, 'I can't sing that.' But Luther Dixon said, 'Just do it for me as a favor.' And as we started doing it the song came alive for me. And then when I heard the arrangement at the actual session, I thought it was fabulous.

"We were fortunate in having Luther," acknowledges Shirley. "The combination was sort of like Bacharach & David and Dionne Warwick." Shirley did a couple of tunes by that team too, most notably "Baby It's You," which made the top ten. "I was never so nervous as when Burt Bacharach was in the studio," she says. "I told Florence, I just can't sing with him in the room. He's a perfectionist, and I was nervous because I thought if I sing one little note that's flat he's going to know it. But he said, 'I'm not going anyplace,' so that was that. Luther, on the other hand, was easy for me to work with. He picked out all our material. He told us when he left Scepter, 'I've given you all I've got. I don't have anything else to give you.' He had to find new people to work with, and we had to find someone else to work with us, and neither one of us was as successful with anyone else as we'd been together."

Nor have the Shirelles been able to mount a present-day recording career. Although they can be found on the same high school gym and oldies nightclub circuit as Shirley, the three are now down to two, since Doris, who had retired once before, recently quit again, leaving Beverly and Micky to carry on the name. But as difficult as it is to conceive of a Shirelles without Shirley (wouldn't it be like a Ronettes without Ron-

nie?), the original group was not named after her. She wasn't
even going to be the lead singer.

"When we were just fooling around in school we were
known as the Pequellos," says Shirley. "I don't know what it
means. But Florence hated that name, so it had to go. She
wanted us to be called the Honeytones, but the others didn't
like that. We thought it was a litle too corny. So we were trying to get a name that sounded beautiful, like the Chantels. We
came up with the Chan-nels, but Florence said, 'No, that's too
close.' One day we were driving home from the office and just
before we got to the Lincoln Tunnel we came up with the Shirelles. We came up with all kinds of things that had that ring
to it. I don't think anyone remembers who actually came up
with the name. It wasn't me. I wasn't the lead singer at that
time, Doris was."

At that time Shirley was still thinking her future career
would be as a beautician. Many of the girls from the Passaic,
New Jersey, projects where she grew up were heading along
that route in the mid-fifties. "I always loved fooling around,
dipping and dabbing and styling hair," she says. "I had a cousin who was going to school for it. She taught me how to do
the curls and all. I always wanted to run a real fancy place,
to be like a Sassoon. As a matter of fact, I did own a beauty
shop. I bought one for my sisters."

But by their sophomore year in high school, Shirley and her
neighborhood cronies would be signed to a five-year contract
with the obscure Tiara Records, owned by Florence Greenburg, the mother of one of their classmates. "We wrote 'I Met
Him on a Sunday' for a school talent show," Shirley recalls.
"One of the girls was baby-sitting and we went by her house
and wrote the song together. We were like a street-corner
group, only being girls we weren't allowed on the corner, so
we'd go down to the basement of Beverly's house, because she
lived in an apartment building and it was all concrete, so you
had the echo chamber effect. We performed it at the show and
the kids went wild over it.

"Florence Greenburg's daughter heard the song and asked

if we'd perform it for her mother. We said, 'Nah, we don't want to sign a record contract, we just want to fool around.' As a matter of fact, we used to hide from her. We'd run around the corner until she passed by. But she kept after us. So we finally went and sang the song at her house. We felt so silly standing there in her living room, singing for her mother, everybody saying, 'You start, no, you start.' "

"I Met Him on a Sunday," a record whose luster has increased with the years, with new luster being added by Laura Nyro's 1971 recording of it, made the charts in 1957. "First time we heard it on the radio," says Shirley, "we jumped up and down. But life still went on the same way, believe me. In school we were just regular people. Our friends were excited for us. When they passed us in the hall they'd say, 'How're you doing? What's your new record going to be?' But as far as really going ape over us, forget it. At first we couldn't do much, anyway, because we weren't old enough to play the clubs. Because we were still in school we could only play Friday and Saturday nights, usually at private parties. After we did 'Dedicated to the One I Love,' we started going out on tour. In our junior year we had to drop out of school and get private tutors."

And for the most part, she's worked ever since, even when the raw edges of the dream began showing through. "When we left Scepter I didn't even care if I worked anymore," Shirley says. "I was very blue. Everybody was blue. We did continue performing, but recording-wise we weren't anxious to jump into anything. By then we'd kind of cooled off. We hadn't had a recording in a while. We weren't a hot item. So everybody wasn't exactly breaking their necks to grab us."

After her show concludes, Shirley is grabbed by a young reporter from the local morning paper, here to do a featurette on the oldies circuit. Although perspicacious in her questioning, the reporter is apparently unaware of the one-time stature of the woman she interviews, back when the reporter was still toddling. But Shirley Alston is too well trained to show her annoyance, too much the professional even to stop smiling. She came up in an era when rock 'n' roll stars were accustomed to working for a living, before the advent of the triple platinum album and the free agent.

"When I was pregnant with my first daughter I worked through my eighth month," she had previously observed. "I did the Murray the K show at the Brooklyn Fox with the belly out to here. So did Doris, when she had her twins. Dionne Warwick used to be my stand-in, in case I got sick. She's the only one I stay in contact with from those days."

These days the grabbings are slim for Shirley and for the remaining Shirelles. The spotlight has swept past them in its relentless search for fresh talent. But in a drafty dressing room, empty of pursuers, she remembers how it used to be. "It was easy to meet people then," she recalls. "Getting rid of them was the problem. They'd recognize us in stores, or on the street. When you'd come offstage after a concert, they'd rush you. Not to tear your clothes off. It was different for girls than it was for guys. Still, if you went out there and you looked attractive and you were singing something they liked, they didn't care if you were married or single, they still wanted to listen to your song. It was up to you to keep yourself from getting involved with anyone out there.

"But nobody had a swelled head. And no big deal was really made about us. We never got the key to the city. One of the girls used to say that all the time. 'They should give us the key to the city.' I said, 'I'd rather have the keys to a car.' "

THE SHIRELLES
TOP 40 CHART SINGLES

1960 "Tonight's the Night"
1961 "Will You Love Me Tomorrow"
1961 "Dedicated to the One I Love"
1961 "Mama Said"
1961 "Big John"

1962   "Baby It's You"
1962   "Soldier Boy"
1962   "Welcome Home Baby"
1962   "Stop the Music"
1963   "Everybody Loves a Lover"
1963   "Foolish Little Girl"
1963   "Don't Say Goodnight and
          Mean Goodbye"

THE KINGSTON TRIO

DAVE GUARD

.■

*I*n the parking lot of the high school the aging greasers stood by their late-model gas guzzlers, trading sips of blackberry brandy washed down with malt liquor. Beyond and below, in the gymnasium of the high school, seats were filling up for a fifties-style dance. With each succeeding circuit of the bottle, passionate and nostalgic anecdotes were imparted concerning the relative merits of such vintage rock 'n' roll groups as the Earls, the Mystics, the Dovells. Injected into this heated discussion, the name of the Kingston Trio hovered in the air like a foul substance, the noxious fumes of New Jersey, say, or the California smog. "Oh yeah," one greaser 1979-model finally sneered, "they're the *beatniks*, right?"

Progenitors of the draft-dodging, pinko, student protestors, the pot-smoking, acid-swallowing, hippie yippies, and the free-love, back-to-nature, love-and-peace, organic, ban-the-bomb, dropout radicals, early folksingers could be found somewhere south of the Top 40 and east of rock 'n' roll. Like modern jazz, folk music snob-appealed to the literate music buff—college educated, fraternally connected, politically liberal. If, in rock 'n' roll, revolution was implicit in the raucous behavior of its juvenile-delinquent mongrel hordes, in folk music it was overt in the lyrics and life-style commitments of its own proponents, the troubadours, minstrels, and left-wing oracles and balla-

131

deers who backpacked, hitched, and Kerouacked across the country, delivering the mail from the bohemian mecca of Greenwich Village to the beatnik nirvana of San Francisco's North Beach.

The influence of folk music on the Top 40—the folk-inspired lyricism and concern, the complex personal and political messages—stemmed from seeds planted in the Dust Bowl by Woody Guthrie in the thirties and nurtured by Pete Seeger of the Weavers, who was banned from TV for his espoused beliefs. Later on, Greenwich Village's own Peter, Paul & Mary would bring Minnesota's Bob Dylan to the attention of the Top 40 masses via "Blowin' in the Wind." Dylan's mythic journey to Woody Guthrie's deathbed would immediately add stature to both legends.

Perhaps softening the Top 40 for such an explosive personality and commentary as Dylan's, the somewhat less radical Kingston Trio evolved from a vibrant San Francisco mid-fifties folk scene, which featured the Gateway Singers—Lou Gottlieb, Travis Edmonson, and black lady lead singer Elmerlee Thomas—who were staples at the Hungry I. "We thought we were almost as good," says Dave Guard, speaking for his northern California singing cohorts, Nick Reynolds and Bob Shane. Together they spiked their folk music with a goodly dose of collegiate ribaldry, some dry-martini wit, native Hawaiian rhythms (both Dave and Bob were natives), and a touch of trendy calypso (the trio took their name from the city of Kingston, the capital of Jamaica). They brought this concoction to the Purple Onion, another San Francisco beer and folk spa, in 1957. "We were sort of trying to sound like the Weavers," Dave admits. "It was really Weavers energy. We liked authentic-sounding stuff." But authenticity would have taken them only so far. The Gateway Singers, with their racially mixed contingent, were finding it impossible to tour. The Weavers themselves, because of their political activities, had trouble getting work. The Kingston Trio, clean-cut and not at all controversial, made folk music palatable to the masses; not the downtrodden masses, but the upscale, striped shirt, rep tie, clip-on-pen middle class.

For the most part, this was a management decision. "We wanted to do some songs from the Spanish Civil War, because they were very ballsy-sounding," says Dave, "but our manager, Frank Werber, said, 'If you do that it will bring all kinds of people around here.' We said, 'What do you mean?' He said, 'Don't even worry about it.' Politically we didn't know what was going on." None of the individual members of the trio was what you could call an avid activist. "We didn't have too much to do with the beat guys. That was an older crowd, a lot of war veterans who were depressed by everything. We felt they were overly bitter. We didn't care about McCarthyism, or whatever else was stifling those people. We were just starting in the world, full of enthusiasm, in the bloom of our cuteness."

If their motives were less radical-chic than those of their predecessors and contemporaries, their ensuing success in the marketplace distanced them even further from their more pristine peers. "We didn't get too much critical acclaim," says Dave. "Critics said we weren't authentic. We didn't feel we could be authentic about anything because two of us were white guys from Hawaii who knew a lot of Hawaiian music, which we sang quite authentically, but in Hawaii they just wanted to hear it from Hawaiians. So everything we played we learned, and we figured everyone else learned the same way, you know, you just pick up what you like. Kind of like the Beatles. Were they authentic? It's all imported, really; music is international." So they came upon their finely polished gems in old albums discovered in the Stanford library stacks, from country and folk music sources, from other groups, and even from the parents of one of Dave Guard's old girlfriends.

"I was pinned to a girl named Katy, and we were going to surprise her one Easter vacation. We went down to see her in Fresno, but she wasn't home. So her folks had Bobby and I come in. They said, 'You know, if you ever have use for this tune, it's a song we've sung since our honeymoon, way back when.' That was 'Scotch and Soda.' When it came time to record it, we couldn't find out who had written it; so I just put my name on it and I figured the guy would come in and claim it, whoever he was, as soon as he heard it on the air. But nobody ever came forward, so we figured we'd saved it, kind of like finding a bottle in the ocean or something. We sent Katy's parents a big bunch of money, since they were our source on the song. You try to take care of your source if you can."

Another famous source whom Dave Guard has long since despaired of locating provided the impetus for the trio to tackle the folk chestnut, "Tom Dooley." Seems they overheard this certain folksinging psychologist one Wednesday at the Purple Onion, doing it as part of his audition for a slot at the club. He didn't get the job. "His name was Tom," says Dave. "I don't know his last name. I wish he'd identify himself. But he wouldn't get any money out of it, because Alan Lomax claims he wrote it." The Gateway Singers had already added the song to their repertoire, but with the Kingston Trio's unique signature, "Tom Dooley" soon became virtually their own trademark. It was on their first album for Capitol, recorded in January 1958 and released the following June.

"I remember it was June 1, 1958," says Dave, "because my oldest daughter was born on the same day." During the summer of 1958, the group played the Hungry I, opening for the mathematician/satirist/songwriter, Tom Lehrer, and pulling down approximately forty-five dollars a man. "We bought a whole bunch of our albums wholesale for seventy-five cents a copy," Dave recounts. "After our set we'd go get dressed, lock the front door of the club so people couldn't get out after the show broke, and sit at a little card table. People asked what we were doing. We said, 'Oh, we're just personalizing albums—you want one?' We sold upwards of seventy-five records a night."

Meanwhile, however, "Tom Dooley," the beneficiary of an admixture of incidents and coincidence, was being heavily played in Salt Lake City, Utah, and Spokane, Washington, largely through the efforts of a lone, prescient deejay who had been fired from one job and had lugged his hot albums up north to the next. Still, those two minor-league towns were hardly enough to hoist "Tom Dooley" into the ballpark of Top 40. That was left, fittingly, to Tom Dooley himself—that is, Dr. Tom Dooley, no relation at all to the Tom Dooley in the song—a man who at that same moment, in another realm of the world entirely was garnering huge amounts of press for his good samaritan deeds in the jungles of Southeast Asia. That the two namesakes should intermingle and mesh in the summer and fall of 1958 surely meant that fate had a hand in "Tom Dooley" 's arrival at the top of the charts, in November of the same year.

"I think it must have been designed that we should support him," says Dave Guard. "We met him once in St. Louis, where he'd been doing some fund raising. He stopped by to thank us. Since the song had become a hit, the money coming in to him had been about ten times higher than usual. But part of the fame of that song came from the fact that there had already been several articles in *Life* magazine about him. He'd been made into sort of a national hero before we came along."

Nine months later, the Kingston Trio were themselves national heroes of a sort, courtesy of their own *Life* magazine cover story. "That firmly implants you in the public consciousness," Dave allows, "but we were already hot before *Life* got onto us." They'd had four albums in the national top ten. They'd headlined at both the Newport Jazz *and* Folk Festivals. Heroically, they'd all walked away unharmed when their rented Twin Beach crash-landed on a turkey farm in South Bend, Indiana, on Friday, March 13, 1959, just five weeks after Buddy Holly perished in a similar accident. "We had a concert to play at Notre Dame that night," Dave recalls. "I think that's what probably saved us." Two days later Bob Shane was married in Washington, D.C.

But all was not fraternal good-fellowship and camaraderie,

beer suds and finger picking. The star trip itself, at least to Dave, was proving hollow as a gourd. "I was the first in the group to get married, so I was married before the group really started getting heavily into things. But there were always a lot of people who wanted to meet you. I saw a lot of one-night-stand-type business, where people would come up to you expecting one thing and not being prepared to deal with your whole personality, only with your media image. So it was like being stampeded for autographs. As soon as they get a foot away, everybody realizes it's a human being standing there, instead of a statue, and they stop screaming and take a look in your eyes, and a lot of their head trips disappear."

There were even hints at discord within the ranks, printed in the media, where Dave Guard maligned the musicianship of his trio-mates. "I started to get bitter that they weren't studying music or anything," says Dave. "I just felt we should keep on pushing to learn all kinds of instrumental techniques and to keep getting better every week. I told them we had a responsibility to the fans to be good musicians and that we should all take lessons to improve our stuff. The other guys weren't big hot students in school or anything; they didn't see how taking lessons would do any good. They had the idea that people liked us for what we were and that's how it was. But they kept their musical ears intact. They brought in some very good tunes in the last stages. And they were true to themselves, in that I don't think they've taken any lessons since."

To compound the strain of being national celebrities and the very model of campus cool, Capitol Records' greedy marketing campaign called for the Kingston Trio to release three albums per year, a strategy that rather rapidly depleted their library of arcane and cherished material. "I liked just about all our first four albums," says Dave. "The first three for sure. I'd say the quality of our work went up, but the enthusiasm for the songs didn't. On the first three albums in particular, we were very interested in all the tunes, those were songs we really liked. Later on we were just looking for tunes that would keep up the quality of the group, that sounded like Kingston Trio songs. Some good tunes would come by, but they didn't grab like the early tunes. Finally, we had to record on such short notice that the tunes would be very respectable, but they just didn't get your heart like the other tunes did." On the other hand, they sold well enough to comprise about twenty percent of Capitol's gross volume one year.

But beneath the claims of lack of musical growth on the part of his mates, beyond the thinning store of acceptable songs, apart from the media histrionics and the pressures of the road and everything else that goes with supporting the mantle of a superstar group, at the core of Dave Guard's growing disaffection from the others was a plaint not unheard in this and neighboring corridors of the Top 40. "Our music publisher was ripping us off," says Dave. "He dropped $127,000 at the tables in Vegas and took it out of our publishing royalties. I had a big check bounce—my writer's royalties just bounced— at a time when you were not supposed to touch those things. When I went down to protest, it turned out that he and our manager were vacationing together in Puerto Rico. So here you are with the cop and the crook in the same boat. I had to get out of the situation."

He shifted his portion of the publishing to Harold Leventhal, Pete Seeger's manager, who also handled the Woody Guthrie estate. This didn't sit too well with Nick and Bob. "They thought I was splitting up the group. But I just couldn't have all this bread disappearing in large chunks." About a year and a half later, in 1961, Dave Guard performed with the Kingston Trio for the last time. "The fans were upset about it," he says, "but to me it was kind of inevitable. I guess the others thought their best shot was to just stay in place. They took an honest look at their chances and saw that getting out of the Kingston Trio would be the end of their money-making days. Ironically, that's pretty much what happened to me." He did, however, net a sizable amount in goodwill severance pay, with which he started a new group, the Whiskey Hill Singers.

"I was thinking of getting something going with Joan Baez in it," says Dave, "because I wanted to have a girl singer. But then I talked to Harold Leventhal and he said, 'Don't touch her, she's too idiosyncratic; she'll never work in a group.' We were at Newport when she first opened up with Bob Gibson and electrified the crowd. Gibson was singing and everybody was kind of nodding, and then she jumped on stage and everybody just emptied backstage; the performers dropped what they were doing and came out to see her, like something really heavy was going down. The next week we were working at Storyville on Cape Cod and she came up with her sister, Mimi, and her mother. Joan asked me, 'What should I do? It looks like I've got a career, and a lot of people are shooting me these hot songs.' I said, 'I think you ought to do just what you're doing, stay in your style.' So I guess she more or less did that."

Instead of Baez, Dave added another powerful and distinctive voice to the Whiskey Hill Singers, Judy Henske, who would have her own brief solo career before retiring to domesticity. It was 1962, and the commercial folk boom presaged by the Kingston Trio in 1958 was blossoming all over the Top 40. Well-scrubbed three- and foursomes, complete with banjo and crewcut, were popping out of dormitory woodwork on seemingly every campus in America in the early years of the sixties. The Highwaymen came out of Wesleyan University with "Michael," a Number 1 song. The Tokens represented Brooklyn College with "The Lion Sleeps Tonight," which also hit Number 1. The Brothers Four, from the University of Washington, had already brought "Greenfields" to Number 2 in 1960. The groves were rife with the sound of four-part harmony, the rich man's doo-wop, with the New Christy Minstrels entering the fray in 1962, along with the more satirical-political Chad Mitchell Trio, whose "The John Birch Society" spent a week on the charts in May. Out of Greenwich Village, where Joan Baez and Bob Dylan were becoming an item, and where every guitar-playing college dropout in the land was immigrating, Peter, Paul & Mary were scoring with their first release,

"Lemon Tree," then their second, Pete Seeger's "If I Had a Hammer," which made the top ten. Earlier in the year, the Kingston Trio, with new member John Stewart, did well with "Where Have All the Flowers Gone?" For folk music it seemed potentially the best of times.

But for a liberated Dave Guard and the Whiskey Hill Singers, it turned out to be the worst of times. "Capitol really stomped on the group," he reveals. "You know, they put out the cheapest kind of master. It got no promotion whatsoever. But on the strength of my being semirespected in the industry, we got a contract to score *How the West Was Won,* and that won an Academy Award. But after seeing how I'd have to fight Capitol all the time, I decided the hell with it." Frustrated, tired, Dave disbanded the group and, with his wife and three kids, moved to Australia. Dropped out.

"I wanted to leave it all behind totally," he says. "I didn't want to have anything to do with the Trio at that time, either. I remember John Stewart wanted to be very friendly and he asked me for a lot of advice, but I didn't want to get involved. It was kind of like graduating from school, you know? I wanted to keep it in the past, otherwise I would have been permanently frozen into it." Australia proved beautifully untouched and tranquil. "It was a lot different than being on the road in a string of motel rooms, where the only food you eat you have to unwrap, the only people you talk to are taxi drivers. No matter how much bread you could make you weren't getting any life value. I decided my values lay with hanging out with the kids when they were young and raising a family. Australia was a bit of sanity, I would say. I did some studio work out there. I got a lot of writing in, and practicing. I had my own TV show. I wrote a guitar method book called *Color Guitar,* where the colors and the notes would be comparable, and I taught that for a while. I wrote a book called *Deirdre,* collecting all the various versions of an Irish legend of two thousand years ago. We stayed until 1968, mainly to raise the kids. We got good property right on the beach at a very good interest rate, and it seemed that World War III wasn't going to be starting there."

The mention of World War III is not an idle metaphor in the vocabulary of Dave Guard. Born in Honolulu, raised on Waikiki Beach, Dave was the son of an army engineer; his mother was an air force commander's secretary. He was all of seven years old at the start of World War II. The attack on Pearl Harbor occurred literally in his backyard. "Yeah, we could see the faces of the pilots as they came over the house. We saw Jap planes going down and antiaircraft fire; it was right there. We watched it for about a half an hour, then cut out for town. We slept under the road in a culvert for at least a week, expecting an invasion." He and his family spent a year in Washington, D.C., before it was safe to return home. In the racially mixed, postwar days, he hung out with Portuguese sailors and the sons of diplomats. His best friend was the son of the Chinese consul. Jazz bands were big on the Islands. He worked at a record shop, haunted the nightclubs, thought he might become a bartender. He was in college in California when he heard Joe Turner, Clyde McPhatter, and Little Richard. He was in grad school when Elvis hit.

Meanwhile, Bob Shane and Nick Reynolds were doing some casual singing at Menlo College, where they were students. As teenagers in Hawaii, Dave and Bob had sung for the tourists on the beach, seasoning their more authentic material with some Las Vegas lounge humor borrowed from the Four Jokers, who frequently played the Islands. In San Francisco, with Bob back in Hawaii after college doing Elvis impersonations, Nick and Dave sang together in a group called the Calypsonians. Eventually they put it all together in Redwood City, en route to the Purple Onion, where they would displace Phyllis Diller as headliners.

Recently there has been talk of a reunion of the original three, plus John Stewart—a sentimental gathering that would make a lot of salt-and-pepper-haired executives feel like sophomores again. "John Stewart is very interested," Dave mentions. "Lindsay Buckingham of Fleetwood Mac has made some positive statements in that direction, and Al Jardine of the Beach Boys has a recording studio that he'd like to get us into." For now, however, the Kingston Trio name is owned by Bob Shane, who bought it from Nick and Frank Werber in 1976. With two new members he's continued to tour, playing before primarily the same people who were fans in the Trio's heyday. They've released a new album on the Nautilus label, out of California, which contains quite a few vintage Trio cuts. "I saw Bobby in 1975," says Dave. "He wanted me to join the group, but I didn't like that particular configuration he had. They were a bunch of sleazy cats; it was just like gang-bang humor, with a lot of drinking onstage and stuff like that. But since then, the guy who took the job I would have had is very good, and Bobby has cleaned up his act pretty well, so it sounds almost respectable now. He learned the hard way. He tried to do it real sloppy, and then he turned around and cleaned it up."

According to Dave, Nick Reynolds, living in Oregon since 1966, raising cattle and Christmas trees, might be up for a reunion, too. And in fact a modified reunion already took place when Dave and his oldest daughter, Cathy, sat in with John Stewart on a couple of cuts from his recent smash album, *Bombs Away Dream Babies.* "We played on 'Coming Out of Nowhere' and 'Run.' On his next album we're going to do a song called 'Sing at the Wheel,' which is a variation of a Druid tune from two thousand years ago—the chorus is—and I added some fresh stuff to it. I'm writing my best songs right now. I guess you'd call them advanced Kingston Trio songs."

If Dave Guard's Top 40 credentials made him suspect to certain folkie purists in the fifties, in later life he's more than paid his bohemian dues. When he returned from Australia in 1968 he got involved with Stewart Brand (of Ken Kesey's Merry Pranksters, immortalized by Tom Wolfe) in putting together *The Whole Earth Catalog.* He's carried the torch for folk music in bands with Mike Settle and Alex Hassilev, in the

Modern Folk Quartet, and in his own Dave Guard and the Expanding Band. Recently on Hula Records he produced a double album of the songs of legendary Hawaiian guitarist Gabby Pahinui. He's also in the process of divorcing Gretchen, his wife of twenty-two years. "Now that we've raised our family, we decided we're two different people."

In 1976 he became a student of the guru Swami Muktananda. "I've cleaned up my whole act behind him," Dave says. "I'm a vegetarian, don't smoke; I'm into a lot of good health, yoga, meditation. I'm studying Sanskrit and Indian philosophy. I'm even into Indian cooking." Indian music, too, has entered his repertoire. "I'm writing out sheet music for all these Sanskrit tunes. It's real good music, real strong. It doesn't sound eerie or anything like that; it sounds like the Russian Army choir—real emotional stuff. The tunes are thousands of years old and they really have a heavy effect on you; everybody sort of leans into them."

In November of 1978 Dave Guard was operated on for skin cancer. A piece of his shoulder was removed. "I had a local anesthetic, but they thought it might be a very extensive sort of thing. So I decided to go through the operation doing the mantra that Muktananda gave me, and I saw golden lights waving around and everything was very cool; my blood pressure and heartbeat were absolutely stable all the way through, from the first reading to the last. So the operating team was very confident that I had my processes under control. I had a follow-up operation about two months ago. They just wanted to make sure all the cancer was gone, and it had been completely eliminated, completely cleaned out. My body was able to clean up all the last remaining little cells. Maybe it was, you know, good health, not having any kind of a depression. If your health is headed toward the good side, then you can handle a lot of these things. That's what kind of really brought me in. I played for Muktananda's birthday celebration, and I talked at this thing he had for Easter and I feel really rejuvenated. I've been looking to see if it's freaky, but I've had no evidence of that. So I'm getting stronger with it all the time."

Folk music, long thought terminally ill by some, buried under the decibels of rock 'n' roll and the detritus of pop culture, has lately been showing signs, like Dave Guard, of rejuvenation. Gone flowers of the sixties back in bloom; seventies seedlings just beginning to sprout—the ageless bcatnik dream incarnate. "Folk music is still pretty vigorous," says Dave Guard. "There's as much now as there ever was. Peter, Paul & Mary just came through town. Arlo Guthrie plays around here quite often. Joan Baez and Mimi Farina are still active, of course, and I think Odetta has been recently seen on the boards. I just talked to Pete Seeger and he's as healthy as ever. He's a fine cat; he was my idol. I had the pleasure of seeing him about a month ago when he came out to San Francisco to play for an antinuclear concert. There were moments during that concert when he looked about twenty-two years old."

THE KINGSTON TRIO
TOP 40 CHART SINGLES

1958   "Tom Dooley"
1959   "Tijuana Jail"
1959   "M.T.A."
1959   "A Worried Man"
1960   "El Matador"
1960   "Bad Man Blunder"
1962   "Where Have All the Flowers Gone?"
1963   "Greenback Dollar"
1963   "Reverend Mr. Black"
1963   "Trouble Is My Middle Name"

NEIL SEDAKA

.■

*T*hey called him "Mr. Moon," this pudgy, moonfaced boy from Brighton Beach, Brooklyn, New York. "I wrote a song called 'Mr. Moon,' and I performed it in the auditorium in Lincoln High School, and there was a riot," Neil Sedaka recounts, twenty-some years removed yet still awed by the memory. "The principal at the time was Abe Lass, and he said, 'I will not let you sing it in the second show.' So the kids at school signed a petition: 'We want "Mr. Moon." ' I was called 'Mr. Moon' after that." And as a result of his newfound popularity he was able to hang out with all the tough kids from Coney Island—a bigtime rock 'n' roller. "Manhattan Beach was the rich area. Brighton, where I was from, was in the middle. The kids from Coney Island were tough; they wore leather. The girls had their hair piled up. My name for her was Frenchie. I think every class had a Frenchie."

It would not be the first time rock 'n' roll had elevated a previously inconsequential adolescent in baggy pants to the level of temporary sultan of the stoop, or the last. But Sedaka, by sixteen, was far more ambitious than your run-of-the-parking-lot greaser. Although classically trained, he'd been writing pop songs since the age of thirteen—when what would come to be known as rock 'n' roll was barely a whisper of static at the far end of the radio dial—an avocation whose impetus was

144

at least in part provided by the timely intervention of a Jewish mother in his building in Brighton Beach.

"Howie Greenfield's mother had heard me playing classical piano in the mountains," says Neil. "She asked me if I ever wrote songs, and I said no. A few weeks later, Howie rang my bell. I recognized him because he lived in the building—3260 Coney Island Avenue. He said, 'I heard you met my mother at the Kenmore Lake Hotel. She said you play piano very well.' I said, 'Yes, I'm studying to be a classical pianist.' He said, 'Well, I write poems. Would you like to try to write some songs?' So we sat down and tried. That was in 1952." Twenty-nine years later, with relatively few separations, they are still writing together.

Some of their earliest collaborations appeared on the album, *Neil Sedaka and the Tokens*, on Melba Records, circa 1955. Notice Sedaka's top billing even then, although he sang lead on only one of the Four Tokens' songs included in the package—"While I Dream." (The remainder of the album was filled with tracks by studio musicians.) Made up of Lincoln High classmates Jay Siegal, Eddie Rapkin, Cynthia Zolotin, and Hank Medress (who would later achieve fame and fortune producing another local boy, Tony Orlando), the group would harmonize incessantly on those Brighton Beach street corners in the shadow of the boardwalk or in Neil's apartment on Coney Island Avenue, where he lived with his parents and his older sister, Ronnie. One of the three other Sedaka-Greenfield tunes, "I Love My Baby," even made Peter Tripp's Top 40 on WMGM, further cementing his high school reputation ("Come Back Joe" and "Don't Go" rounded out the young team's initial contribution to song literature).

In 1961, the Tokens, sans Neil, Eddie, and Cynthia (but with the addition of the Margo brothers, Mitch and Phil), had a Number 1 national hit, "The Lion Sleeps Tonight." Back in 1955 the original Tokens had ridden the subway to local glory on Brooklyn's lucrative wedding and bar mitzvah circuit, ears meanwhile glued to the radio, where rock 'n' roll was beginning to breach the static. "There was no FM at the time," Neil recalls, "but at the end of the AM dial you could hear rhythm and blues on the Jocko show. And then Alan Freed would play it on WINS. There was a mambo show, Bob 'Pedro' Harris. Mambo and latin started at the very same time as rock 'n' roll, and they were kind of neck and neck for a while. Being from Brighton, we used to buy La Playa Sextet, Machito, Tito Puente. I honestly was not into Elvis. His vibrato annoyed me. I was into Fats Domino, Chuck Berry, and Little Richard. I remember when I first got a tape recorder, I would tape right off the radio—put the radio in the kitchen, and tape off the Alan Freed show.

"The first rock 'n' roll record I heard was 'Earth Angel' by the Penguins. It was in Andrea's Pizza Parlor on Coney Island Avenue. I think I was sitting with Carole King [her name would have been Carol Klein at the time] and we were having pizza and it came out of the jukebox. I said, 'Oh, this is marvelous!' It just knocked me over. And that's who I started writing for, groups like the Nutmegs, the Harptones, and the Penguins."

As a backdrop for city boy meets girl, rock 'n' roll from the outset was unparalleled. "Musical people would always throng together," Neil says. "I met Carole either on a street corner or through a mutual friend, I don't remember, but she would follow me around every time I appeared at a wedding or a bar mitzvah. Then we started going out socially, and we were very close for a couple of years, until she met Gerry Goffin. She had a group, too, called the Cosines. Her mother told me that I was a bad influence on her, because she would neglect her schoolwork to write songs and to chase me from bar mitzvahs to weddings. And my mother would say, 'Why do you like her?' Because she wasn't particularly great looking in those days, and she was a chain-smoker. To my mother that was the worst, a sixteen-year-old girl who's a chain-smoker. I said, 'I'm intrigued with her.' "

Meanwhile, Sedaka was venturing as a solo singer into the

primitive wilds of the record business. "I was being managed by a comedian, Lenny Maxwell, who heard me playing piano up in New Hampshire at Lake Tarlton. I made some piano and voice demos at Phil Ramone's studio." Ramone would one day number among his production credits million-selling albums by Simon & Garfunkel, but in those days his studio was in his apartment. Sedaka recorded "Snow Time" and "Laura Lee" there. "Unbeknownst to me, Lenny Maxwell went to Decca and put a rhythm section behind them. He came ringing my doorbell a few months later with a finished master." Nothing came of that session, but songs by the Sedaka-Greenfield combination were being put to wax during the same period by discerning producers like Jerry Wexler and Ahmet Ertegun of Atlantic Records, for established rhythm and blues artists like the Clovers, the Cardinals, LaVern Baker, and Clyde McPhatter. Sedaka's "Passing Time," was the flip side of a major r&b hit, "In Paradise," by the Cookies. Neil also recorded several sides for Harry Finfer's Guyden Records in Philadelphia, including "Fly Don't Fly on Me" and "Ring-a-Rockin' Music."

" 'Fly Don't Fly on Me' was a terrible song," Sedaka relates. "I didn't make any money on it, just the excitement of hearing it on the radio. I heard it on WINS. I was at my friend Armand Sorrentino's house in Brooklyn. 'Oh my God, that's my voice!' That was just overwhelming. And then another time I was sitting with a friend watching Dick Clark's "American Bandstand" at three-thirty in the afternoon, and all of a sudden Dick said, 'Here's a new artist singing "Ring-a-Rockin' Music.' " I fell off the chair. And Dick had me on the Saturday night 'Beech Nut Show' as an unknown with 'Ring-a-Rockin' Music'—not one of the greatest songs of our time."

This moderate flurry of attention surely stoked his already flaming pop-star fantasies, but it was hardly the stuff upon which a middle-class Brooklyn boy, an aspiring Leonard Bernstein, could base a career. So Neil steadfastly took the BMT up to the Juilliard School of Music in Manhattan, where he'd been in attendance since the age of fifteen (going to the prep school on Saturdays for two years before graduating to full-time status), to pursue his other destiny. "My teachers there were kind of amused by rock 'n' roll," he says. "It was something they didn't know too much about. They'd have me go into one of the rehearsal pianos. They'd say, 'How do you write these songs?' 'What is an Elvis Presley?' For me it was a way of having fun. One teacher asked, 'Can you develop, can you grow with this music?' I said, 'I don't know; it makes me feel good.' "

Ultimately, the fantasies began to score some serious runs on mundane existence, knocking practicality and the regimented life of the classical musician out of the box. "I'd been reading *Billboard* and *Cashbox* since I was fifteen," says Neil. "I'd read them from cover to cover as I rode to school. I would look at, I think it was the top sixty then, and I would live it. I remember once scratching out the name of the artist who had the top song and writing Neil Sedaka there, just to see how it would look. I bought 'Love Is Strange' by Mickey & Sylvia, and on the label I scratched out the writer and put Neil Sedaka. After so many years of living it, I could taste it, hear it."

That was in 1957. By the end of 1958 he did hear it, taste it. It would sound glorious, at first and for years it would taste as terrific as it had in all his fantasies. "Howie and I met Doc Pomus at 1650 Broadway. He told us Don Kirshner was opening up a new firm. I played 'Stupid Cupid' for somebody at Hill and Range, and he said, 'Well, I'm not sure.' So I went upstairs to Don Kirshner's office—they'd only been in business a few days—and they flipped. I played 'Stupid Cupid' and about nine other songs. They wanted to sign us up as staff songwriters." This was the soon-to-be legendary Aldon Music (a partnership of Al Nevins and Don Kirshner), a publishing company that would turn Tin Pan Alley rock 'n' roll into high pop art, largely through the efforts of such songwriting *menschen* (many of them Brooklyn neighbors of Sedaka and

Greenfield) as Carole King, Gerry Goffin, Barry Mann, Cynthia Weil, Jack Keller, and Tony Orlando.

Al Nevins was with the group the Three Suns, who were signed to RCA. The chance for Sedaka to record his own songs on that label was an added enticement which Al threw into the offer to sign immediately with Aldon Music. Yet the team demurred. They'd been burned too many times in their short career. They had seen their tunes, ruined by poor productions, cast upon the murky waters of pop and r&b music, 1955–58, with little tangible success. And neither man nor songwriter can live on fantasies alone. Greenfield, twenty-two, was employed at National Cash Register. Sedaka, nineteen, was making plans to spend the summer working in the Catskills at the Esther Manor Hotel (where he would eventually marry the boss's daughter, Leba). Instead of committing themselves to a long-term contract right away, and instead of leasing the song to the publisher for the standard year in which to get a recording, Howie and Neil had an alternative suggestion. They'd let Aldon have the songs for three months, and if they could get one on the charts in that time, the team would sign with them. Kirshner, of course, asked for four months. But actually, all it took was one day.

It was a hot afternoon in May 1958, when Kirshner took Howie and Neil to meet Connie Francis, who was riding high with successive Top 40 items—"Who's Sorry Now," which had gone to Number 4 earlier in the year, and "I'm Sorry I Made You Cry," which was nudging into the middle thirties even as they circled the block in Kirshner's car, waiting for her to emerge from the beauty parlor. At her home the two fledgling songwriters ran through their repertoire without a pause. The last song they played was "Stupid Cupid." This one she wanted to hear again. She heard it again, and then pronounced, "That's my next record."

And so it was. Released in July, "Stupid Cupid" went to Number 14 on the big board; Sedaka & Greenfield went with Aldon Music, beginning a professional relationship with Don

Kirshner that remains intact today. As good as his word, Al Nevins got Neil Sedaka signed to RCA as a vocalist by Steve Sholes, their A&R chief, the man who'd signed Elvis. By November of the year, still nineteen, Sedaka would have his first release on RCA, his first chart record since the days of neighborhood acclaim on Peter Tripp's show. It was the top-fourteen smash, "The Diary."

As Neil tells it, "The Diary" almost never came to be. "I was signed to RCA Victor for several months and I still didn't have a record. Al Nevins wanted me to wait for the right song. He was very smart. I had written 'The Diary' for Little Anthony & the Imperials, but when I heard what they did with it I was despondent. That's when Al Nevins said, 'That's going to be your first record on RCA Victor.' First I went with a big string section at the RCA studios on East Twenty-fourth Street. I was shaking in my pants I was so nervous. And the record came out very sterile. I told Al and Don I didn't like it. They asked me what I wanted to do. I said I'd like to get Armand Sorrentino, Howie Tischler, all the kids from school and bring them into it. And that's exactly what I did. Forget about the violins, forget about the chorus and people who could read music. I brought in my friends, and they sang on it. There were three tracks and three speakers, with me singing live at the piano."

While the record took off, Sedaka reported regularly to the song stables of Aldon Music, where he honed his craft. "I always worked the same way," he says. "I wrote the melody, or a good part of it, and Howie would stand there and write the lyrics at the same time. I would sing them out, and if they didn't fit, he'd revise them. I learned to write a song in every beat, in every feel. I would study the records on the radio so I could play the top-ten hits fluidly. There were assignments. Connie Francis would ask for a specific kind of song. She wanted a song called "Frankie"; we gave her a song called "Frankie." There was a movie she was up for, *Where the Boys Are*; we wrote "Where the Boys Are" for her. I was in the office writing every day." During those halcyon years there were more songwriters than cubicles, each working on the same assignments, the melodies intermingling, the egos bouncing off all thirty-six walls. "We used to wait until we all came back with our demos and everybody used to sit in the office and listen. I remember Carole's demo of 'Will You Love Me Tomorrow.' It was marvelous. I came in with 'Breaking Up Is Hard to Do,' and Barry Mann and Cynthia Weil said it was very mediocre." It only turned out to be Neil's biggest hit, in 1962 reaching Number 1, and going top ten again in 1976 in an updated interpretation.

"I was a teenage hit. I bought a 1959 Chevy Impala convertible. I could walk on Bay One of Brighton Beach. I can't tell you the excitement when my voice came on the radio and everybody had the same station on all across the beach."

Oddly, however, during these years he hardly toured. His managers, Kirshner and Nevins, kept him deskbound. "They were afraid to have me work too much," says Sedaka. "I had a lot of good years, but no one knew what I looked like. I wasn't in too many of the teenage magazines. They went for the very pretty boys; I was too skinny. I was handsome, but I didn't have the thing Fabian or Frankie Avalon had. They were in movies already. I was just a voice. I never did the Dick Clark tour. I was on "The Ed Sullivan Show" once. I played the Copacabana once. I played the Brooklyn Paramount with Alan Freed and Murray the K, had beer bottles and lit cigarettes thrown at me, four shows a day. I played the Steel Pier in Atlantic City. Then came the bow tie and tuxedo—everybody wanted to be Bobby Darin. So I played the Twin Coaches, the Holiday House. They didn't want to take a chance on me bombing in the United States, so my first gigs were in the Philippines, Brazil, and Japan."

Sedaka claims the distinction of being the first teenage rock 'n' roller to ever appear in Brazil. This was in 1959, when "Oh Carol" was Number 1 in a variety of international markets. "I headlined with a group of Brazilian musicians who didn't speak English. We had arrangements for eight songs. That was the extent of the act."

Looking back over the years, the charts, the numbers, Sedaka can recall names and positions much in the same manner an old ballplayer, one of the Boys of Summer, perhaps, can remember, down to the inning and the score, his opposite-field home runs with more than one man on. " 'The Diary' just missed top ten. My second record, "I Go Ape," was a flop in this country, but a hit in Europe. My third record, "Crying My Heart Out for You," was a total flop. 'Oh Carol' started the string. Then there was 'Stairway to Heaven,' 'Run Samson Run,' 'You Mean Everything to Me,' 'Little Devil,' 'Happy Birthday, Sweet Sixteen,' 'Calendar Girl,' 'Breaking Up Is Hard to Do,' 'Next Door to an Angel,' and then they died away." Sedaka's recap contains a slightly selective memory lapse, for, during the stretch he's recalling, from 1959 to 1962, he also released "Sweet Little You" and "King of Clowns," both of which failed to make the Top 40. Nevertheless, of the eleven records he had out in those four years, six made the top ten, and "Little Devil" just missed, at Number 11—an impressive streak.

Through it all, Neil still lived in Brooklyn. "I retained the same friends," he says, "I felt like a big fish in a small pond and I liked that, it was good for my ego. I felt uncomfortable being with celebrities. I never really indulged myself or had money so to speak. My mother took it all. She knew a gentleman who became my manager. I bought myself one car every year. When I traveled it was for singing; I never went on vacations, was never into clothes. I did it for the power and the fame. I liked being recognized when I went into a place where they knew me from 'The Ed Sullivan Show.' But I stayed the same old Neil; I never changed."

But something was changing. Every day the wheels of the Top 40 spun, and someone who was previously accustomed to being a winner could just as suddenly find himself on the outside looking in. "It was gradual," says Neil, speaking of the knowledge that the streak was over, maybe for good. "After 'Next Door to an Angel' was 'Alice in Wonderland,' which made top twenty. Then 'The Dreamer,' which only got into the forties. And my brother-in-law at the time—married to my sister—said, 'You know it's going to end.' I said, 'I know it,' but it was not easy to accept. At that time Neil Diamond became popular, and his parents were right across the street. They owned a clothing shop on Brighton Beach Avenue called Diamonds. And everybody said, 'Well, whatever happened to *you*? Neil Diamond is doing so great.' But little by little the records stopped, and I got over it," he says softly. "I got over it."

He was twenty-three at the time, just married, at the point in a young man's life when the future, if still indistinct, is definitely ahead. His was retreating, dancing backward into the past, vanishing into the air like a radio station sucked off the currents as an automobile ceaselessly blunders west. "I had made a great deal of money, but a lot of it went astray because of mismanagement, because of bad investments. I had an accountant, Allan Klein, who made me buy a building in Birmingham, Alabama, for $150,000. That went down the drain. I didn't have charge of my money. I was married to my wife and we were living in a fantasy. My money, my entire life was being run by Donnie Kirshner, Al Nevins, my mother, and my mother's friend."

Dutifully, maybe desperately, he clung to the songwriter's trade. When Don Kirshner sold Aldon Music to Screen Gems in 1963 for a few million clams, Sedaka and Greenfield, along with Carole and Gerry and the rest of the crew, changed offices, moving east to Fifth Avenue. Ironically, this postchart period turned out to be one of his most prolific in terms of writing. "I wrote with three lyricists, five days a week," says Neil. "I was writing with Carole Sager, Howie Greenfield, and Roger Atkins. I said I could write like Paul McCartney, and I did write like Paul McCartney, but it was very hard to get records when I wasn't singing the songs. I made one record for

Colgems, which was a part of Screen Gems, called 'Rainy Jane,' produced by myself and Howie Greenfield, and it was terrific. I heard it once, I think, on WNBC. The only time I'd hear myself on the radio was when an oldie would come on. So I felt, well this is it, I'd better get resigned to the fact that I had my shot and it'll never happen again."

Through the rest of the sixties Sedaka penned singles sporadically, but his songs did show up on albums by Johnny Mathis, Peggy Lee, the Partridge Family, and the in-house group, the Monkees. He also had "Working on a Groovy Thing" and "Puppet Man," which were top-twenty items for the Fifth Dimension in 1970 . . . the first signs of what was to be a long and grueling, often humiliating climb back to the very top. Carole King's landmark *Tapestry* album of 1971 was another harbinger that the wheel was about to spin again.

"When I heard the album it blew me away," he says. "I said, 'Oh my God, that's my style, the piano, the voice, the whole approach to melody—we grew up together.' And I begged Donnie Kirshner to let me do an album for RCA. I wrote probably the best collection of songs I ever wrote in my life. I was going to do it like Carole, with a small group. But Donnie called me in, and he said, 'You're a classical artist. You have to have a big symphonic thing.' And he called in Lee Holbridge, who's a brilliant arranger, and the songs came out sounding like magnificent things that should have been on the Broadway stage. The album was too classy, and it was against the market; RCA was not about to promote it. So *Emergence* was a flop, and it shattered Howie Greenfield and me, and we split up for two and a half years."

This was no mere professional parting here, after twenty years. This was childhood's end. "It was very sad," Sedaka recalls. "Howie moved to California. Just before he left we wrote two songs; one was called 'Our Last Song Together,' the other was 'Love Will Keep Us Together,' which I think was kind of like his plea. We both cried."

For the performer and the lyricist, the tears, like the tides and the tables, would turn, but not before a painful hejira to the lower depths. Greenfield faced down a two-year silence. Sedaka pocketed his ego and knelt before imposing club owners, more unknown than he'd ever been as a teenager. "The original record of 'Oh Carol' had been re-released by RCA and was a hit in England. So I picked up my wife, my two kids, and Mary the housekeeper, and we moved to London. I got a job at a real toilet in Manchester." Then he was introduced to an area group called Hot Legs, who had a studio in Stockport. "They were marvelous," Sedaka recalls. "I sat down and recorded a whole album with them. I spent $6,000 and recorded an album called *Solitaire*. It had 'Solitaire' on it, "That's Where the Music Takes Me,' 'Standing on the Inside.' And I brought it back to Donnie, and he said, 'Well, I'm not sure.' He got RCA to put it out—on a shoestring. Nothing happened. But I knew when I heard the record that I was on the right track."

His second album in England was entitled *The Tra La Days Are Over*, also recorded with Hot Legs, who were by then better known as 10cc. It marked another step forward along the comeback route. But the light at the end of the tunnel had to come from America; his self-enforced exile required the kind of hero's welcome only a hit record could provide. And who else could give him and his career the kind of boost that was needed—a blurb, a pat on the back—but his chain-smoking buddy from the old neighborhood, his songwriting stablemate turned L.A. superstar, Carole King. She was divorced from Gerry Goffin, but hopefully still funky enough to remember Andrea's Pizza Parlor.

"I saw her when I went to L.A. to record another album for England," Sedaka recounts. "She said, 'What are you doing here?' Like she owned L.A. I said, I'm recording at Clover studios,' and she said, 'Oh, that's nice,' almost resentful. She didn't want to know of the past, or have anybody infringing on her territory." The album, *Laughter in the Rain*, produced the single of the same title that was a smash in England (and which in 1975 became a Number 1 song for Sedaka in the U.S.).

"By that time Elton John and I were pretty close," Sedaka says. "We had met many times at Bee Gee concerts; we were both friendly with Maurice Gibb. One night at my apartment in London we had a big party and I took Elton and [his manager] John Reid aside. I said, 'I'm frustrated. I have a hit in England. I'm now a concert artist in England. You've got to help me.' It just so happened they were in the process of opening Rocket Records. I said, 'Don't pay me. I don't want any money. Just put out a compilation album, some of the things I did with 10cc, some of the things I did in L.A. All I want is your endorsement.' And that's what he did. The album was *Sedaka's Back*, and he wrote on the jacket, 'Neil Sedaka's songs are great . . . ' "

The next time Sedaka went to Los Angeles, it was to headline at the Troubadour. "I took over the town," he modestly exclaims. "Every producer in town was there.' The comeback was complete, the hero was home. "I wanted it with a vengeance," Sedaka says. "Donnie Kirshner said I would never make it again; that drove me. My old manager said I'd never make it again; that drove me. Carole King; that drove me. I knew I was good, and I spent hours at the piano. I wasn't afraid of it. My voice was a great help to me, too, because I knew that nobody could sing those songs like me, nobody. The critics in L.A. couldn't believe that anybody could write and sing with such enthusiasm, with such spirit, and with this vengeance."

Sedaka, it appears, would agree with Frank Sinatra about the loveliness of the second time around. "It felt much better," Neil concurs. "I was now managing my own affairs. Everything creative was in my hands. I had a more well-rounded performing career. I broke into Vegas. I had that experience opening for the Carpenters, where I blew them off the stage. Leba and I, when we went to England, had to call on radio stations. I had to *schlepp* to these places. I had to lower myself, humble myself. Now I appear on TV practically whenever I want." And the crowning touch, the icing on the cake, or, if you're from Brooklyn, the foam on the eggcream, was the BMI award for Most Performed Song of the Year, on the Captain & Tennille's recording of "Love Will Keep Us Together."

Sedaka palms the award proudly. "It was the dream of a lifetime. I mean, I'd been going to that BMI dinner since I was a kid. I got six awards in one year, including the Most Performed Song of 1976." He looks down at the award, then corrects himself, "1975, I mean, beating out 'Rhinestone Cowboy.' I was afraid of 'Rhinestone Cowboy.' "

The slight error in chronology cools the moment, reminds him his valiant comeback is even further down the pike than he'd recalled. He resumes his seat on the couch, rather like the 1979 New York Yankees. He muses a while on that song, laden with sentiment, symbol of his odyssey in rock 'n' roll. "I was such a smash," he says, "why didn't I put it out myself as a single? After 'Laughter in the Rain' came out, I had ten other songs on *Sedaka's Back*, but I picked 'The Immigrant,' because it was a beautiful song and a beautiful record, and it made number 22—after a number 1."

He leans forward, at the edge of a painful conclusion. "I just can't last more than three or four years on the chart. I just can't. The last three years my records have stopped selling, and I'm eating my *kishkas* out. Thank God I have a performing career. But, being a record person, I feel very frustrated at this point. I have two albums out on Elektra Records that have not sold, and I'm discouraged.

"Even though I have fame, I have money, I have a wonderful family, I feel very unhappy, because it's always the records that have driven me. It becomes a way of life—what am I on ABC, what am I on KHJ? Unless you see it go up on the charts, you've failed. I was lucky enough to have it all those years; perhaps it'll never come again. Perhaps I don't have that creative spark anymore. Perhaps I'm not hungry enough. I could be bigger. I could be richer. But I just started writing again last week, after not writing for almost a year, and it scares the hell out of me."

NEIL SEDAKA
TOP 40 CHART SINGLES

1959	"The Diary"
1959	"Oh Carol"
1960	"Stairway to Heaven"
1960	"You Mean Everything to Me"
1960	"Run Samson Run"
1961	"Calendar Girl"
1961	"Little Devil"
1961	"Happy Birthday, Sweet Sixteen"
1962	"Breaking Up Is Hard to Do"
1962	"Next Door to an Angel"
1963	"Alice in Wonderland"
1963	"Let's Go Steady Again"
1963	"Bad Girl"
1975	"Laughter in the Rain"
1975	"The Immigrant"
1975	"That's When the Music Takes Me"
1975	"Bad Blood"
1976	"Breaking Up Is Hard to Do"
1976	"Love in the Shadows"
1976	"Stepping Out"

Update: In 1980 Neil Sedaka once again hit the Top 40 on a duet with his sixteen-year-old daughter, Dara, entitled "Should've Never Let You Go."

BRENDA LEE

▪

Seated on the back steps of the stage at the Canaan, New Hampshire, county fair, waiting for her show to commence, Brenda Lee is requested by a fan to pose for a snapshot in front of his 1960 Buick. He bought the car the same year she had her first hit record, "Sweet Nothin's." Beneath the familiar bouffant hairstyle and frilly junior-miss dress, Brenda seems to have hardly aged in all those years. She leans against the fender, thirty-five-going-on-sixteen, laughing. Yet a closer look reveals the road-lines etched into her skin, nearly thirty years worth. In the immediate distance, flannel-shirted farmboys wielding chain saws race from log to log in a contest of speed and power. It is this log-sawing exhibition that has forced the delay of the Brenda Lee Show.

But Brenda doesn't mind. As the interminable lull grinds on, she is a model of patience, a pro. When it comes to dealing with the realities of the pop-star life, Brenda's undoubtedly seen it all, endured it all. Perhaps never quite a chain-saw competition, but there were certainly scary times in South America. When she finally gets to open her set some forty minutes later, belting out her 1966 hit "Coming on Strong," it's clear the little girl with the big voice—Miss Dynamite—has lost none of her power and desire. It could be 1965, when she played a command performance for the Queen of England. It could be another county fair, in Milwaukee, with Ricky Nel-

son as the opening act, in front of fifty thousand fans. That today it's a crowd just barely one-tenth of a percent as big, in
New Hampshire, under a threatening sky, hardly seems to
trouble her.

Patience has always been one of Brenda Lee's virtues—the
patience of a trouper who played Las Vegas when she was
eleven years old. She was performing for ten years before she
had her first hit record in America, patiently releasing about
a dozen bombs, semisuccesses here, hits in England prior to
the Buick song, "Sweet Nothin's," which brought her world-
wide fame at age fifteen. More recently, when she suddenly
found herself excluded from the Top 40 by the purveyors of
psychedelica in the late sixties, she took a sabbatical from the
recording studio rather than waste her talent bending to the
marketplace. She returned in 1972 with a brand-new country
music career, and a string of country smashes from 1972 to
1976. When Owen Bradley, her long-time producer, retired
from MCA Records in 1976, Brenda left the label too. She
stayed home a little bit more with her daughters, Julie and Jo-
lie; she bided her time. Though a number of songs meant for
Brenda Lee went on to become hit records for other artists,
Brenda didn't let that phase her. When the time was right, she
knew she'd be back where she belonged. And in 1979, when
MCA got a new president, she was coaxed into the fold once
again.

The first thing she did was to get herself a new hairdo, a
new look, trading in the image of the sixteen-year-old girl-
next-door she'd toted from state to state ever since she was
eleven years old for a more mature, contemporary style befit-
ting her age and immense track record. The next thing she did
was to come up with another hit single, "Tell Me What It's
Like," moving up the country charts, followed by an album,
Even Better. After three years, patience rewarded.

About the only time in her life or her career—almost one
and the same thing—that Brenda Lee showed the least bit of
impatience was in her decision in 1963, at age eighteen, to get
married to Ronnie Shacklett, a contractor six months her sen-

ior who was then employed by his father. Brenda's manager,
Dub Allbritten, was dead against it. Brenda's mother, Grace,
didn't attend the wedding. "I think if it had been left up to
Momma and Dub, I wouldn't have ever married," comments
Brenda. "Dub was a very possessive fellow, like a father. He
didn't think I was old enough, first of all, although I was almost nineteen. And being in the music business, I had matured
mentally a bit quicker. He was also very skeptical of everybody
who liked me. He wanted to make sure they liked me for *me*,
and not for anything else." Allbritten was understandably concerned about what this might do to her career. Such matters
as image and availability, the opinions of boys in corduroys
and girls who read *Teen Screen* magazine in the early sixties,
were still of vital moment to the ascent of any singer. But
Brenda wasn't at all worried. "At the time I was married I had
the Number 1 record in the world. I didn't think it would be
that dramatic, because my image wasn't one of a heartbreaker.
I wasn't an Annette; I was the little fat girl your mother didn't
mind you playing with. It wasn't like the beauty of the neighborhood was getting married."

Even had she known that her Number 6 hit earlier in the
year, "Losing You," would represent her last appearance that
high on the national charts, it's doubtful Brenda would have
changed her mind. "I was ready for marriage," she asserts. "I
needed the stability and I wanted a family, because I didn't
have that much of a family life."

Her natural father died in an accident when she was seven,
and Brenda Lee Tarpley, already singing professionally with a
gospel group called the Masterworkers Quartet, was pressed
into service to support her family—two sisters and a brother.
Both before her father's death and after her mother remarried,
the family moved around quite a bit, usually in whatever direction Brenda's singing career dictated. By the time she was
eleven, she would have lived in Atlanta, where she was born,
Cincinnati, Augusta, Georgia, and Springfield, Missouri, and
be every bit the mile-wise TV, nightclub, and state-fair veteran.
She'd been on John Farmer's "TV Ranch" in Atlanta, had

sung on deejay Peanuts Faircloth's "Record Shop" program in Augusta and on Red Foley's "Junior Jubilee," out of Springfield, where she was the hostess for six months, eventually moving up to Foley's nationally syndicated country show, "The Ozark Jubilee," where further attention was paid to this girl they were starting to call the new Judy Garland.

Along with Red Foley, Brenda credits a mention by influential New York columnist Jack O'Brian with helping to launch her toward her first contract with Decca Records, in 1956, the same year Elvis Presley began rocking on RCA. Her early efforts were far less successful than the King's, however, perhaps because her record company didn't really promote the rock 'n' roll side of her. They were after a sweet, shy, child popstar prodigy, not a tough little mama with a bourbon voice. "I wanted to do other songs, but they said it wouldn't be believable to the public because of my age," says Brenda. So there was the Hank Williams country classic, "Jambalaya," followed by "Christy Christmas," and "Fairyland." In 1957 she made the charts for the first time, with "One Step at a Time," barely missing the Top 40. But the follow-up, "Dynamite," couldn't get past Number 72. So, with Las Vegas behind her and several Perry Como shows under her belt, twelve-year-old Brenda, her manager, and her mother packed up and went to Paris.

"I went over there originally for three weeks and I wound up staying three months," Brenda recalls. "I went to school in Paris and learned to speak the language fluently." She played the Olympia Theater with Gilbert Becaud, author of "Let It Be Me." She had a hit single in Europe with a song based on an old mountain adage, "Let's Jump the Broomstick." According to Brenda: "When two people in the mountains wanted to get married, they didn't do it by preacher or minister, they just jumped over a broomstick and that meant they were married." Throughout the remainder of the fifties while she was in school in Nashville, she returned to Europe in the summers. For five years in a row, from the ages sixteen to twenty

(1960–64), she won the British trade paper *New Musical Express*'s award for Best Female Vocalist.

When school was in session, she tried to restrict her performing schedule mainly to the weekends. During the week she was a dedicated student at Maplewood High, with an extracurricular load that was nothing less than heroic, including, by her account, the debating team, the cheerleading squad, and editing the school newspaper! This all changed when the hits started coming at age fifteen, and the family picked up and moved to Los Angeles. Brenda went to professional school and had a tutor who accompanied her on the road.

"I guess it had to be done then," says Brenda, "but it wasn't like going to regular school. I had the same academic success I would have probably achieved in public school, but it was not a normal atmosphere for me." Her relative lack of education is something that gnaws at Brenda far more than her relative decline at the top of the pop charts. "I had one year of college by correspondence. I wanted to continue, but I didn't have the time. Now I just finished sending my last sister through college. Everyone has a degree except me, and I was the one who wanted it so bad. Maybe one of these days I'll go back."

Brenda settled for fame and fortune, although she didn't come into the substantial part of her fortune until she was twenty-six, owing to Tennessee's interpretation of the Jackie Coogan law (which withheld from underage performers a certain percentage of their earnings until a state-determined majority) and her manager's tight purse strings. "I never knew what I was making," says Brenda, "and I didn't ask, as long as my mother was taken care of and my brother and sisters. I was allowed to buy certain things. I bought my mother a house. But I didn't need anything, other than clothes to go to school in. After I got married, my husband supported us, I didn't."

At fifteen Brenda entered the world of rock 'n' roll. It was via the Dick Clark tour, accompanied by her mother, her manager, and her tutor. "I was well chaperoned until I married," she recounts with a smile. Still, like Jo-ann Campbell before her, she was the only girl on the bus, also the youngest. "Fabian was about two years older than me. My best friend on the tour was Duane Eddy, and we're still very close." By 1960 rock 'n' roll had achieved some minimal acceptance; the atmosphere had lightened a bit from the dark ages of the fifties. Yet there were still problems to be encountered, especially in the South.

"Chubby Checker was on the tour, and he couldn't do the southern states," says Brenda. "We'd have to meet him back in the North, and that was kind of hard on him. I always felt so sorry for Chubby. We'd all wave good-bye to him. 'See you in a couple of days.'"

Aside from age and gender, many other things separated Brenda Lee from her contemporaries. Unlike most of those raucous teenagers out for a joyride, flashing their latest hit record around as if it were a draft card, a symbol of manhood and maturity, Brenda was a seasoned performer with a growing repertoire and eyes much wider than the next sock hop. She'd already played Vegas; she was gunning for the Copa in New York. Those rock 'n' rollers with their crew cuts or their duck tails must have seemed like schoolboys to her, terribly uneducated and insecure.

"Back then you worried about your first hit," says Brenda. "Then you didn't worry about the second, because the second was going to ride on the first to an extent. It was the third one you really worried about. If you didn't get the third one, you were either out of the business or it was like you were an embryo all over again, because nobody cared what you had out. It was, 'Well, what are you doing now?' You had to prove yourself every time you put out a record. This created a feeling of desperation among some of the people, because they didn't know what to do with themselves, how to pace their careers, or strive for longevity. I guess I would have felt that way too, if I had been in the same predicament, but fortunately I was not.

"Most of the ones who survived, like myself and Paul Anka and a few others, knew, or their managers knew, that you had to have a tremendous amount of respect for the business, or you couldn't stay in it. You couldn't be accepted, you couldn't even make it, if you didn't remember who put you there, and that was your audience, the deejays, the writers—people like that."

This essentially happy-to-be-here attitude, which was anathema to many rebellious rock 'n' rollers of the time, may be what ultimately kept Brenda's career going for so many years, what helped ease her transition to the country charts. She was always thoroughly professional. She toured constantly, even when she wasn't riding a hit record, even when she had no current record out at all. It was an attitude ingrained in her from the beginning.

"My manager would never let me listen to other singers," she says. "He didn't want me to start trying subconsciously to sound like them, or take little tricks away from them. But once my style had already been formed, he made me sit down and listen to everything—and I still have everything—that Frank Sinatra ever recorded. Not so much for singing, but for phrasing. The only other thing that was pounded into my head from the time I got my manager was articulation of words. And then choosing good material. I had all the control on that, because I don't think you can sing a song unless you pick it, unless you feel it. I'm basically a lyrics singer, and I tried to pick songs that would not become passé; that I still could do in front of audiences ten, fifteen years later. You have to think in terms of if you don't have another hit record for a while, then you can still do those things and you won't be out of the public's eye."

So Brenda Lee—in attitude, experience, and personality—was relatively sheltered from the pandemonium that was rock 'n' roll, 1960–63. After one circuit, she left Dick Clark's bus: "Too grueling." She put together a band, including such top Nashville sidemen as Buzz Cason and Wayne Moss, that would stay with her for years. Fairly quickly she began to temper her sets with soft, feminine ballads like "All Alone Am I," "I'm Sorry," and "I Want to Be Wanted." When the frenzy started to ebb, she got married, and shortly thereafter gave birth to her first daugher. Only her early rockers and shouters, obscure songs like "Bigelow 6200" and "Ain't That Love," indicate what may have been the last flickerings of her own rebellious soul that soon deferred to her more conservative, practical nature.

"Rock 'n' roll had so much adverse publicity," she notes. "Ministers were burning records and real 'uptown' folks whose opinions were respected were putting it down. Teenagers were rebelling and parents couldn't understand it." She says this from a distance, as an entrenched member of the working class who didn't have time to indulge in such shenanigans. "There was a whole sexual revolution going on, but only in the minds of girls. And then, when Elvis came along, here was a guy you could scream and yell at and get your frustrations out in the open.

"I was a friend of Elvis's, and I was a fan. I can't say that I went to his concerts and screamed and went all crazy, but maybe it was because I knew him." They'd met, in fact, at the Grand Ole Opry, that country music institution and bastion of decency, where they were both appearing for the first—and last—time. "I was the first person to use drums at the Grand Ole Opry," Brenda claims. "They weren't allowed, but they let me use one little old snare drum. Elvis and I did the show right before he went to Germany in 1957, and I was billed over him. I couldn't believe that. I still have the poster. It keeps me humble. It keeps me real humble."

Though she didn't get to know him well, she did come close enough to Elvis to see how he choked on his name, was suffocated by his fame, and the hangers-on who pumped it. It was something Brenda swore she'd never let happen to herself. "Well, I think he got caught up," she says. "He couldn't get out. There must have been some place where he could have gone, you know, without people knowing; a place where he could have been alone and been himself. I don't think Elvis, especially after he got out of the service, was ever allowed to be Elvis. He lost sight of who he was. Sometimes you do that. I've been to the point where I was saying, 'Who am I? Who is Brenda Lee? Is that just a name? When I go on stage, is that who I am? And then who am I when I come off?' Those are questions that unfortunately you have to ask yourself in this business, because you can get caught up in things. If you're unable to answer them, you can find yourself in pretty hairy condition."

Brenda Lee found herself, in 1967, at the age of twenty-two, unable to answer certain basic questions about the drift of her career. She'd run the gamut of TV variety shows, played the Copa, conquered Europe and South America, knelt before the Queen of England, and she'd headlined over Elvis and Ricky Nelson, but she'd lost her lease on the top ten (though not the top twenty). To prevent summary eviction from the charts entirely, she decided to step back and survey the territory.

"Music changed," she says. "It changed the first time in 1964 with the Beatles, then it did another change in 1967 with psychedelic acid." This last phrase is uttered with the obvious discomfort for the nomenclature of a nonbeliever and nonindulger, a person of a chronological age to have been among the original flower children, but in reality a generation apart—settled, middle-of-the-road, twenty-two-going-on-forty-five. "There was just no place for me," says Brenda, "and I wouldn't prostitute myself to do what was happening."

Actually, Brenda goes way back with the same Beatles who were the spear carriers of "psychedelic acid." In the summers of her adolescence spent in Europe, she played some dates with them, when they were backing up Tony Sheridan in Germany. "I didn't associate with them that closely," she says. "I was a teenager and they were older. They didn't talk a whole lot to anybody. They were kind of cocky, but in a nice way." She wasn't surprised by their ultimate success. "You can knock the Beatles all you want to. You can knock the way they looked, knock what they said, but cannot knock their musical genius. They started a whole new wave of comprehensive intelligence in music, and there's no way you can knock that. When I worked with them they were going under the name of the Golden Beatles. They were fantastic writers, and they had most of their songs even then. They recorded the weirdest way I've ever seen. To go to a session with them, you'd go into the studio and you'd stay for a month. John thinks up a line and then they may go home to bed. And then the next day Paul thinks up something and then they put music to it and then they do it. It could take them up to a week to do one song.

"I tried to get them a contract with Decca Records at the time," Brenda recalls, "but Decca didn't want to know about them."

From 1964 through the remainder of the sixties, the Beatles played their pipes and led a generation into Strawberry Fields (not quite Forever). Meanwhile, Brenda Lee, several years younger, had lost her audience in that same generation. In 1969 she released a ballad, "Johnny One-Time," which is one of her personal favorites, but it failed to dent the Top 40. So she withdrew again, this time until 1972. She had a baby daughter to care for. Perhaps she considered retiring for good during this period.

Brenda says no. "Retiring would be traumatic for me. I was still working on the road some at this time, I just didn't record. Now that hurts your career a little, because you're more or less out of the ballgame if you don't have some product to put out there. Fortunately, it didn't hurt mine all that bad, although it certainly didn't further it any. But I would rather not have anything on the market than something that's not up to what I think it should be. if you just keep putting stuff across program directors' desks, pretty soon they start to say, 'Oh Lord, here's another dog.' And then when you do get something good, it makes it that much harder to get it played. I got out before that started happening to me. If it had, it would have killed me."

In low moments Brenda can take solace in what she's already accomplished in her career. She enjoys discovering a

new list or poll which confirms her place among the top all-
time record sellers, such as the one she found in *Newsweek* in
1977, noting the top twenty artists of the past twenty years,
with Brenda at number seven, behind Elvis, the Beatles, Fats
Domino, and Ricky Nelson, ahead of Connie Francis. Or another one, revealing which five artists best survived the coming
of the Beatles. Her survival in the music business makes her
rejection in other realms a little easier to bear. In 1962 she
tried to parlay her rock 'n' roll success into a movie career,
like Annette and Frankie and Connie before her. "I don't talk
about it a whole lot," she says of her inauspicious debut in *The
Two Little Bears*, starring Eddie Albert, Jane Wyatt, Jimmy
Boyd, and "Introducing Brenda Lee." Says Brenda, "If I got
any good reviews, I didn't see them. Although the picture
went instantly toward the filmic equivalent of the thirty-nine-
cent rack, Brenda definitely had the acting bug. She played in
summer stock versions of *Bye Bye Birdie* and *The Wizard of
Oz*. In the contract she signed with Decca in 1963, she was
guaranteed two movies with Universal. The movies were never
made. "They paid me anyway," says Brenda, without a trace
of rue. She's been writing poetry since the age of ten. "I was
encouraged to write songs," she says, "but I'm not interested
in that." A book of these poems, however, remains unpub-
lished.

Since 1971, when her manager Dub Allbritten died, Brenda
has been overseeing her own affairs out of Nashville, where
her two daughters, fifteen and ten, have grown up, and where
her family life, at least, has remained firmly rooted, But the
seventies have been erratic for her career. From 1972 to 1976
she was a mainstay of the country charts, a grand dame on the
"Hee Haw" show. Then, in 1976, she left her label and went
three years without a record. She continued to tour a solid
twenty-eight weeks a year, but many of these dates involved
such grueling arrangements as hopping into a borrowed bus,
motoring all day and all night from Nashville to White River
Junction, Vermont, arriving at six in the morning for an after-

noon and an evening performance in Canaan, New Hampshire, before a desultory crowd, many of whom still see her as the sixteen-year-old girl-next-door.

"I've been working out a new deal with MCA," she said in the trailer behind the stage, "but nevertheless I haven't been able to record, and I missed 'Here You Come Again,' " naming a recent hit by Dolly Parton. "Barry Mann [writer of the song] sent that to me and I held it for eight months. Then I finally had to give it back to him. I also had 'I'd Really Love to See You Tonight' and 'She Believes in Me'—I was going to do it as 'He Believes in Me.'" That she had to pass on those songs, all of which became huge national hits, is surely frustrating—but just the fact she was offered them at all, in her then ice-cold condition, was both a tribute to her past and a promise for the future. And although her new album has yet to cross over from the country to the pop charts, and although she might not fully realize it, there are plenty of people who still believe in Brenda Lee.

"I guess there are a lot of girls out there who probably listened to me," she says, "maybe cut their teeth on some Brenda Lee records." Country singers Tanya Tucker and Barbara Fairchild are mentioned, and the seventeen-year-old rocker Rachel Sweet. Then Brenda chimes in. "I was really proud with Stevie Nicks of Fleetwood Mac. I love her, and I finally got to meet her. I said, 'I'm really embarrassed, but would you sign my autograph book for me?' And she put down, 'To my greatest inspiration.' And I thought, she's heard of me, Stevie Nicks of Fleetwood Mac. I couldn't believe it."

BRENDA LEE
TOP 40 CHART SINGLES

1960 "Sweet Nothin's"
1960 "I'm Sorry"
1960 "That's All You Gotta Do"

1960 "I Want to Be Wanted"
1960 "Just a Little"
1960 "Rockin' Around the Christmas Tree"
1961 "Emotions"
1961 "I'm Learning About Love"
1961 "You Can Depend On Me"
1961 "Dum Dum"
1961 "Fool Number One"
1961 "Anybody But Me"
1962 "Break It to Me Gently"
1962 "Everybody Loves Me but You"
1962 "It Started All Over Again"
1962 "Heart in Hand"
1962 "All Alone Am I"
1963 "Your Used to Be"
1963 "Losing You"
1963 "My Whole World Is Falling Down"
1963 "I Wonder"
1963 "The Grass Is Greener"
1964 "As Usual"
1964 "Think"
1964 "Is It True"
1965 "Too Many Rivers"
1965 "Rusty Bells"
1966 "Coming on Strong"
1967 "Ride, Ride, Ride"

Update: Brenda followed "Tell Me What It's Like," which reached Number 8 on the country singles charts, with "The Cowboy and the Dandy." She followed *Even Better* with *Take Me Back*, doing well on the country album charts. She seems to have recovered her country audience.

LITTLE ANTHONY & THE IMPERIALS

ANTHONY GOURDINE

■

"*B*ob Dylan said in *Rolling Stone* some years ago that rock 'n' roll ended with Little Anthony & the Imperials." This is Little Anthony speaking, who just turned forty in January 1981. "The era really ended around 1960, two years from the time we had 'Tears on My Pillow,' but we were the last group in the rock 'n' roll era. All the rest of our hits—'Shimmy Shimmy Ko-Ko-Bop,' 'Going Out of My Head,' 'Hurt So Bad'—were in the sixties."

This is not nearly the extent of their credentials. "We bridged the gap between the races," says Anthony. "We were one of the first black rock 'n' roll groups to be totally adopted by a white audience. The Shirelles never reached the peak we did. They were making records, but the unique thing about Little Anthony & the Imperials was that we became a great performing act. We spent eight years in Las Vegas and Lake Tahoe. No other group in the history of Las Vegas made such an impact. We were one of the highest-paid working groups. We played the top places in the country. And we were the only ones in the whole world who came out of that era and went in that direction. We set the stage for everybody else. Gladys Knight & the Pips saw us; the Temptations came in and watched us very carefully."

With the assimilation of Little Anthony & the Imperials into the culture at large, post-1964 rock 'n' roll dropped its last pretense of innocence, the other blue suede shoe. Was it revealing its perhaps fatal flaw in its drive for respectability and approval, with all the compromises that would imply—a guile the equal of its ambition? Or was it merely growing up? Whatever, coming on the heels of the arriving Beatles, Anthony's departure for Vegas symbolized the polarities of a generation gap: on one side a culture based on certain flowery precepts; on the other show biz, and everything implicit in that pejoration. Years later the gap would be all but closed, the flowers wilted, show biz trumpeted as "survival." But back then it was still a matter of concern to rock 'n' roll fans straddling two worlds as their era ended.

"We hadn't heard of the Beatles," says Anthony. "We saw a picture of them and we laughed at the way they looked. When we heard that record they made, we said, 'Come on, that'll never make it. We were very hot at the time. We had 'I'm on the Outside (Looking In),' and we were at GAC, a big agency that was handling the Beatles' American tour in 1964. It turned out that one of the groups they had asked to work with was us. We said, 'We're not going to work with a group like that. Open the show? They should be opening the show for us!' Murray the K called us up and he said, 'Are you guys crazy? They're going to be the biggest group in the world.' We said, 'Ah man, we're on top of the world too. We don't need that garbage.'

"We blew that. We blew a lot of things when we were young."

They almost blew Little Anthony & the Imperials. Twice. In the early fifties, Anthony Gourdine, the youngest of four brothers, lived in the Fort Greene Projects in Brooklyn, dreamed of being an actor or a ballplayer, and ran around in street gangs with Clarence Collins and other members of a singing group called the Chesters. "They weren't social clubs," Anthony says, "they were real gangs. If you were hanging out with the guys on the street, you automatically were part of the gang. I was in the Chaplains. I was what you call a part-time Chaplain. I didn't give my all to it. I was the type of guy who was too busy singing, too interested in that. But when I need it, like in school, when I needed the protection of a gang, I did cling close to them. But when that was over, I got as far away as I could, because I didn't want to be in any gang. But where I lived it was a thing you fell right into."

The Chaplains may have protected the frail Anthony, but the Chesters represented his future interests. Beyond that, they were his buddies. They hung out; they slept at each other's houses; their parents all knew each other. Just about the only thing they didn't do together was sing. Anthony was with another incipient rock 'n' roll ensemble, the Duponts. "You know in high school they had the lunchroom, right?" he continues. "We'd go down to the lunchroom and that's where we'd sing. We'd be sitting there eating lunch and somebody would start off, and then somebody else would come in and harmonize. We had some pretty good singers at Boys High— a baseball player by the name of Tommy Davis, Richie Havens. We used to sing day in and day out, walking down the street. Nobody had record contracts on their mind.

"When I was with the Duponts there were a lot of records being made. Just like any teenagers we all had girlfriends who would love the songs. And we would say, 'Boy, I'd sure like to make a record. I wonder if I'm good enough to make a record?' You'd figure it sounds good in the street, sounds good in the subway, sounds good in the projects; maybe it would sound good on a record. I wonder how you make a record? And then somebody would say, 'They make records in New York City.' 'Where in New York City?' 'I don't know, over on Broadway somewhere.' So one of the guys in the Duponts knew somebody who knew somebody in the business, and they said come on over. But there were so many hustlers and liars then, just like today. We'd meet a guy who said he was the head of a record company. We'd say, 'Wow!' We'd sing for the guy and he'd say, 'We'll call you,' and that kind of thing. And then we'd sing for someone else."

Eventually one of these leads panned out. "We heard from a guy named Paul Winley. He got some money from somewhere and we made a record. We recorded a song he wrote called 'You.' He was a friend of Dr. Jive—Tommy Smalls— on WWRL in New York, which was the major r&b station. In those days it was still 'race' music; it was just beginning to be a national thing. We got that one station to play the record, we heard it on the radio, and we thought we were kings of the world. Then we found out that he was a big crook and so we left him. We couldn't sue anybody then; the business was so loose at that time. You used to sign contracts just about on toilet paper. We thought we had some money coming, but we really didn't. Only one station played it. It probably sold twelve copies."

Meanwhile, Clarence Collins was trying to persuade Anthony to defect from the Duponts and join the Chesters. He assured him that the Chesters had made their contacts in the city, too. Good ones, like Richard Barrett, who had graduated from the r&b group, the Valentines, to the high offices of Gone Records, the manager then of the Chantels, Frankie Lymon & the Teenagers, and a new group out of Cincinnati, the Isley Brothers. Barrett had expressed an interest in the Chesters, but only if they could come up with a lead singer. But Anthony remained cautious. Even though the Duponts had released a record, had appeared on an Alan Freed show at the Brooklyn Paramount with the Platters, the group's efforts had come to nothing. "He talked to me for about a year," says Anthony. "Finally I went over to hear the Chesters sing one day, and they sounded perfect. I said, 'I'd like to be with you guys.'

"We sang wherever anybody would listen to us—on street corners, subways, in community centers." At the same time they made themselves familiar with the music industry's natural habitat. "Every day we would go over to 1650 Broadway, which was a famous building where every record company in the world had an office. Down the street was 1619 Broadway, the Brill Building, where all the writers, composers, and publishers were. Everything was in a five-block area—rehearsal studios, record stores. The main store was the Colony. You knew you had a hit record if your song got played outside the Colony. In those days you could make a deal with them and sell it right there."

Richard Barrett wasn't the easiest man in the world to get an audience with. But the Chesters were not to be denied. "We even followed him one time to a big show where the Chantels were on with Danny & the Juniors, and we waited outside in the cold for hours and hours." Exhibiting the fortitude and endurance that would ultimately separate them from nearly everyone else in rock 'n' roll, they kept their eyes steadfastly on the main chance. "This went on for about a year. Finally one day we just went up to his office and stayed there. He'd pass by us and we'd say, 'We just want to sing for you.' Clarence said, 'We got a lead singer, his name is Anthony. You've got to hear him.' And I'm sitting there with my head down, shy.

"Finally he told us to come into the office and we sang a song that Ernest wrote called 'Just Two Kinds of People in the World,' and Richard stopped in his tracks. I wasn't leading the song, Ernest was—I was singing the high part, the tenor. Richard called in George Goldner, who was president of Gone Records. George heard it and said, 'I'm going to record you guys.' We were very excited, because in those days George Goldner was the man."

Their first recording session also marked Anthony's songwriting debut, on a collaboration with Ernest Wright, "Cha Cha Henry," which was to be the flip side of their first release, "Just Two Kinds of People in the World." But George Goldner had other ideas. "He said there was a particular song he wanted us to sing, and he played it for us. We weren't too impressed with it." Nevertheless, they were in no position to argue. So they agreed to work on "Tears on My Pillow" with Goldner and Barrett. "We had to think of the simplest background we could, so we took the background from 'Earth Angel.' It was the quickest thing we could learn. But when I got in there on the microphone it didn't come out as George wanted it, so he came out of the booth and stood in front of me and he said, 'Listen, why don't you sing like you talk?' And that's what I did."

The finished product became a high-priority item in the company. "Everybody put all their energies behind it," says Anthony. "George Goldner said to us, 'If this isn't a hit record, I don't know what records are.' " At which point they got an early lesson in the prevailing rules of the game. "It was not until the record was done and everybody knew it would be a hit that they called us in and said we've got to change your names. They said *the Chesters* didn't have any zing to it. They wanted something special. We were really outraged by that. Then the publicity man suggested the name *the Imperials*, like the car. In those days it was probably far better to own an Imperial than a Cadillac. It was a regal name; they wanted something regal . . . and there already was a group called the Regals."

Soon after the record was released, Alan Freed began referring to Anthony as "Little Anthony." "I was a little bit taller than Frankie Lymon, but Alan knew I was small because he remembered me from the Duponts. The original record had the Imperials on the label, but Alan Freed changed our name on the radio. When he said 'Little Anthony & the Imperials,' something happened. A lot of people, first of all, thought I was a girl. And then they thought I was a little-bitty boy. For a long time people thought I was twelve, thirteen years old."

Another thing that happened was that the rest of the Imperials began to feel upstaged. "At first they were upset," admits Anthony, "but as we began to get bigger and more popular they started realizing that it was for the best." Recognition came quickly, especially for Anthony. "We did a major local TV show called "The Jocko Show," on Channel 13 in New York. I think we were seen on that show by just about everyone in Brooklyn. People in school would come up to me. 'You're Little Anthony? You're the same Gourdine who . . . ' In school they called me by my last name. That was the beginning.

"After high school my instinct was to go to college, but we started working right away. Our first major show was at the Uptown Theater in Philadelphia in 1958. Before we knew it we were playing in Hawaii, kids who'd never been past New Jersey." But the trip was far from smooth. "I would be a liar to say that there was no hostility in the group." says Anthony, "but we also loved one another. We'd been raised together. Ours was a deep relationship. Whatever animosity there might have been was overwhelmed by the love."

Before long rock 'n' roll saw to it that this love would be severely tested. After a string of bombs (among them "So Much," "A Prayer and a Jukebox," and "Wishful Thinking") followed the top-five "Tears on My Pillow," Little Anthony developed a bad case of the star complex. "The reason why was very simple," he explains. "There was a lady. I won't give her name because that wouldn't be fair to her. I don't know if the woman's alive or dead today. But I was very young at the time and she impressed upon me that I would do far better if I went out as a single. So I took her advice and left the group in 1961." One of the last songs they did together was to mark a moderate return to Top 40 acceptance, "Shimmy Shimmy Ko-Ko-Bop," a ditty which ranks as Anthony's all-time *least* favorite song. "I didn't want to record it," he says. "I thought it was the dumbest song I ever heard, and I still think so today. I don't even like to sing it onstage, but I do."

Even with that tune nudging the name of Little Anthony & the Imperials back into the consciousness of their public, neither end of the byline could make much profit. "I released records, the Imperials released records, but none of them did anything. Meanwhile I took jobs singing wherever I could. But the clubs wanted to hear the old music. Can you imagine that? I was already an oldie but goodie. That's the irony of rock 'n' roll, because you're dealing with kids twelve to fourteen years old. They grow up and their tastes in music change automatically. Rock 'n' roll never really had the loyalty that pop music has. Very few people got that loyalty. One was Elvis Presley, and that's why he was so unique, because he was the only one, really. Jazz has a loyalty, country music has it, r&b, but not rock 'n' roll. Today you're a king and a heartthrob for young girls, tomorrow it's someone else."

On the other hand, pop, jazz, country, and r&b rarely inspired the same manic adoration, the same hell-bent intensity, making that moment spent in the spotlight both searing and divine. "I was literally stripped of my clothes in Toronto, Canada," Anthony recalls with pleasure. "I was in the hallway of the Queens Auditorium, underneath a stadium jam-packed with screaming girls. I was with either Fabian or Frankie Avalon, who said, 'Let's take this side door here.' We were on our way to the bus, walking down this long corridor and thinking we were cool because everything was quiet. Then all of a sudden we looked down the corridor; about a quarter of a mile in the distance there were millions of girls coming at us . . . and they were screaming. We turned around and ran the other way, and there was another pack of screaming girls. We said, 'Oh mercy!' and they attacked us. They took all of my top shirt off. I don't know what they did to Fabian.

"It happened again at the Apollo Theater. I went down into the audience to sing to a girl and, I don't know, I must have hit a note or something, and the girl fainted. Then the rest of the girls in the audience stampeded and tore my clothes off. We took our lives in our hands in those days."

So it seemed that it was all over, even before the echoes of those screams had faded. It seemed that Anthony Gourdine was destined to repeat his father's experience. An itinerant jazz musician, the old man had been forced to give up the dream and opt for a career in maintenance when family obligations set in. By 1963, without a group, without a song, Anthony was married and himself a father.

Here once again his friends from the old neighborhood, now known as the Imperials, bailed him out. "We were still friends, even when we broke up," Anthony says. "We were hanging out at each other's houses. I was going to gigs with them. People were always asking us to get back together. Ernest had an apartment at the Mohawk Hotel in Brooklyn, and I used to go there all the time. One day we just said, 'Hey man, let's do it.' Two of the original members, Tracy Lord, the tenor, and Nathanial Rodgers, the bass, had left. We got Sammy Strain, who'd been with the Chips, to join us, and he was with us for fifteen years. Now he's singing with the O'Jays.

"The Imperials had developed in the business much quicker than I had. They worked with Richard Barrett, who helped them a lot. They started playing the Catskills and getting a taste of nightclubs. Their repertoire changed; they started going after pop songs, learning modern harmony, studying the Hi-Los and the Four Freshmen. A gentleman by the name of Kenny Seymour sang with them for a while. He now does work in Europe as an arranger. He was brilliant at teaching them four-part harmony. Richard Barrett is now the manager of the Three Degrees, and the toast of Europe. He can't get arrested in America.

"The Imperials had become fine performers. But I was still going around doing 'Tears on My Pillow.' I stayed very stagnant, very rock 'n' rollish. What they did was to teach me what they were doing. I fell into their rhythm; they didn't fall into mine. As soon as we started rehearsing we knew it was going to be magic. We worked so much it was unbelievable, We worked everywhere, especially in the New York area— whenever there were teenagers or college kids. I think we were the forerunners among rock acts to play colleges. That was the audience that really dug us."

At the same time there were still people around who remembered Little Anthony when he was but a tiny member of the Duponts. Late in 1963, nine months into their new incarnation, Teddy Randazzo, once one-third of the Three Chuckles, got in touch with them. The costar of the film *Hey, Let's Twist* was also a producer and songwriter for the fledgling Don Costa Productions. Teddy thought he had a song they might want to do. He sat down at the piano and played them "I'm on the Outside (Looking In)." While they were in the process of putting this tune together, Alan Freed's successor at WINS, Murray Kaufman, soon to be known as Murray the K, got wind of their reunion. He immediately put them on one of his shows at the Brooklyn Fox, second billing to Johnny Mathis.

"It'll be something I'll always remember for as long as I live," says Anthony. "The theme of the show was: The Triumphant Return of Little Anthony & the Imperials. We walked out onstage and there were so many people, from Brooklyn, Queens, the Bronx, and all you could hear was screaming. They just loved us, and we didn't know we were loved." Within weeks "I'm On the Outside (Looking In)" was completed and released. "Murray the K was the first to break the record," says Anthony, "and it was a smash."

The leap to Las Vegas, however, represents more than the innocent conjunction of popularity, love, and momentum. Elvis got there via Hollywood, packaged in a gold suit with tassels. Paul Anka got there, possibly on the strength of Frank Sinatra's rendition of his "My Way." Many other rock 'n' roll originals passed through town and were either turned off by the smell of success, or turned away by the pop establishment. Very few black rock 'n' roll groups got as far as Carson City. Little Anthony & the Imperials, up from the slums, surpassed more than their forefathers with this move, and broke new ground in which to plant their funky roots. As he would put it, "Our persistence wore down their resistance."

In retrospect, Anthony can see how the road to Vegas practically started at his door in Brooklyn. "Our knowledge of music as individuals was far greater than a lot of the kids at the time. I was influenced by my father and his records; I was really raised on jazz and pop music. I came up listening to the

Ravens, the Inkspots. Clarence and I were the biggest fans of classical music. I think growing up in New York City, we were exposed to a lot more culturally than other groups. Richard Barrett was also instrumental in our fate. He always instilled in us his discipline about performing. A disciplined person is a disciplined person. He will be exactly what he's going to be and that's it. The discipline came as the years passed. We became a disciplined group. I'm a professional performer today. I know what I have to do to go out and entertain people. From the very beginning of the Imperials we were influenced by certain things. I was a fan of Sammy Davis. I mean kids didn't know who Sammy Davis was, and I was looking at him. I was loving Nat Cole. Then Richard Barrett taught us the business, and as we grew and we began to see the fruits of it, we realized that this was the thing to do. And we went about doing it, while ninety-five percent of the other acts stagnated. A singer who was just as advanced as we were was Frankie Lymon. He could have been one of the great performers of our time, but he never developed because he had internal problems. You're living in a world of illusion, where you're put on a pedestal. You're made to think you're something you're not when the world falls at your feet. Rock 'n' roll is one of those areas of music where you can today be on the corner doing nothing, and then write a song and become a hit. It's not like pop music where guys have to struggle inch by inch, and by going through that struggle they grow slowly and are able to cope with a lot of the success. These kids came out of nowhere and the next moment they were on top of the world, and then all of a sudden the crash came."

As far as Anthony is concerned, he was preparing for the crash right from the outset, even if he wasn't aware of it. "The Imperials were the last group to work the tail end of vaudeville. We worked a thing called the chitlin circuit, all black theaters—the Regal in Chicago, the Apollo in New York, the Royal in Baltimore. Here's the kind of people you'd play with: there'd be a juggler, a comedian, tap dancers like Stumping

Stumpy, Buddy Briggs, Coles & Atkins. All the things you see in Motown in the Temptations, Gladys Knight & the Pips, the Jacksons, all those steps—that's Charlie Atkins. We came up with people like Flip Wilson, Moms Mabley, Redd Foxx, and from them we learned comedy timing. We retained 'Tears on My Pillow,' all our records, but we developed into a very sharp act by learning all the tricks we picked up in the theaters. We never say it immodestly, but we always feel like we were a blessed group."

Las Vegas—the Rainbow—beckoned the first time in 1965, soon after "Going Out of My Head" brought Anthony and his buddies some long-awaited top-ten recognition. But it was nothing compared to a month at the Flamingo Hotel. "We understood that we had made a big, big jump," says Anthony reverently. "We knew we had to be good." And they *were* good. But not great. "We didn't fail," he says of that initial gig, "we just didn't succeed. There was a group called the Checkmates working at Caesar's Palace who were performing at the level we should have been at. We were doing a lot of the vaudeville things, very show business, very slick and classy, but that was the era when they were just getting down into disco, and that's what the Checkmates were doing. We learned a lot from them.

"We played the Flamingo again, and we were a little stronger, but we still had not reached the point where we wanted to be. We'd be playing to a half-full house; the Checkmates had standing room only. You couldn't get in to see them. All the stars were going over there. That's how you know you're doing well in Vegas, when your peers come to see you." In their early Vegas days, Little Anthony & the Imperials had a very unlikely number one fan: Ann-Margret. "She was very young and very shy," Anthony recalls, "and she always had laryngitis. She'd come in all the time and we'd sit there talking show biz." It was not until 1970 that the group was able to relocate from the Manhattan area, scene of their scuffling youth, to Las Vegas, the Emerald City of their pop maturity. Paired with

Redd Foxx or Bobby Vinton, Little Anthony & the Imperials went from rhythm and blues to blue chips.

"Real show business takes years," Anthony advises. "A lot of the young acts that were coming up didn't realize the kind of sacrifices you have to make in order to reap from it. The time is not your own. You sleep, eat, and think show biz." In return, the rewards are not insubstantial. "When you looked out in the audience, you'd see everybody from Connie Stevens to Johnny Carson. There were times I'd look up from sitting with someone like Muhammad Ali, and say to myself, 'Oh man, here I am from Fort Greene, running in gangs up and down the street. I'm sitting next to these people, people of stature; I'm in their homes. I'm talking to Sammy Davis! Here's the guy I loved to watch and we're talking like we've known each other for years.' "

Once entrenched in Las Vegas, even the loss of their recording career was a blow that could hardly pierce the Imperials' new identities. "There was a war between Don Costa Productions and United Artists," Anthony relates, "and we were caught in the middle. We didn't record for about ten months, and by that time we lost momentum. But, really, we didn't lose anything, and we ended up being the highest-paid group without records." But not far beneath that show biz veneer, there still beats the heart of a Top 40 man. Anthony will even admit that the lack of a hit was behind the group's second, and final, breakup.

"The group didn't break up," he corrects, "it came to an end. We had gone as far as we could go musically and professionally. We could still work all the time, but that was not our motive. Our motive was to keep developing. I knew it years before it finally happened; I knew it was coming. It was a matter of trying to delay the end, hoping that somehow a hit record would come."

It's possible, then, that Anthony & the Imperials might still be making music together today had they been able to come to terms with producer Thom Bell in 1974. "Because of a difference of one point on a record deal, one percent, we didn't do 'You Make Me Feel Brand New.' " The song was subsequently released by the Stylistics and went to Number 2 on the charts. "It was ours," Anthony sighs. But a tale like that only confirms to Anthony how fate was really calling the tune in the dissolution of the once-and-nevermore Chesters, in September 1975.

"We had one of our greatest performances that night, too, in Nassau in the Bahamas. But all day we were in tremendous turmoil, arguing with each other, arguing with our manager. When it gets to that point, something's really wrong. It's like a marriage that has become bitter. We looked at each other and we said, "It's the end, man, it's the end for us.' " Completing this divestment of the past, this move toward the uncertain future, Anthony was also divorced and remarried in 1975. "Show biz did not cause the demise of my marriage," he insists. "My wife enjoyed every moment of it. The children enjoyed every moment of it."

Free to pursue other areas of his creativity which had remained dormant—like acting, writing, and dancing—Anthony has moved, since 1975, slowly, cautiously, inexorably into theater, TV, and films. In 1978 he came out publicly as a Christian. "It was always there," he says. "But saying what I am is a recent development." Stating his case more clearly may be the album he's currently working on for B. J. Thomas's company, Trinity Productions, exclusively devoted to contemporary Christian music. "It's not gospel, " he says with a laugh. "It's pop music with Christian lyrics. My songs are uplifting. They're about the love of people and of God. I like to think they're inspirational."

About as inspirational as the journey, perhaps, of the little kid from the slums who was able to save his skin, who got out of this rock 'n' roll alive when it started crumbling all around him, who wound up rubbing knees with the show biz giants. "There's no rock 'n' roll anymore," Anthony announces in triumph. "Rock 'n' roll is gone. It's all pop music. The hard-rock area is left for a few cult-music people. But I have devout fans to this day, people in their early forties, mid-forties, who will follow me wherever I go."

LITTLE ANTHONY & THE IMPERIALS
TOP 40 CHART SINGLES

1958 "Tears on My Pillow"
1960 "Shimmy Shimmy Ko-Ko-Bop"
1964 "I'm on the Outside (Looking In)"
1964 "Going Out of My Head"
1965 "Hurt So Bad"
1965 "Take Me Back"
1965 "I Miss You So"

Postscript

"JO-ANN"
1958
by the Playmates

*A*nyone even slightly consumed by rock 'n' roll during his teenage years probably had his own "Jo-ann," some obscure but cherished all-time favorite song, a memento of a slightly warped sensibility, all the more cherished for its obscurity. Recorded by the Playmates early 1958, "Jo-ann" wasn't much of a song, I admit it. For historical significance and influence, insights, epiphanies, or original arrangement, look elsewhere. It was not one of the textbook gems of rock 'n' roll (although it does sport one of the more durable and evocative alto sax solos of 1958, the model for the sax solo in "Born Too Late," by the Poni-tails, another maudlin classic released six months after "Jo-ann"). But I'm not talking textbook perfection. I'm talking about the power of the Top 40 single, even as wielded by one of its lesser representatives. For as disposable as "Jo-ann" may have been, to me it sums up the meaning of the Top 40 era, as well as my entire adolescence, both of which culminated with the coming of the Beatles.

Urging my fever for the song "Jo-ann" to a somewhat higher pitch was the presence in my life of a real Jo-ann (named Jo-ann), this apple-cheeked cherub I'd coveted from afar since 1956. She also appears in literature, my Jo-ann does, in my novel entitled *Me, Minsky & Max*, showing up in the guise of Arlene Foster, like so:

"Back in the 6th grade there was one Arlene Foster, a rather buxom brunette with a slight overbite, who provided me with my functioning definition of desire. . . . It was a cool day in October, when kneeling at my desk in my brand-new corduroys, attempting to pick up the pencil I dropped, I happened to gaze straight up Arlene's dress, all the way to her baby blue panties, as she stood chatting with her friend at the next desk, sublimely oblivious. I must have hovered there over my yellow number 2 Eberhard Faber pencil, dazed, swooning, tying my shoelaces, policing the area, all the blood in my body crammed into my skull, for a solid three minutes, or until Arlene finally moved on. Although I'd never spoken to her, and never would, although she'd soon be supplanted in my fantasies by Elaine Scaduto, that moment in and of itself was so searing that it had burned a permanent place in my sexual history book, and ever since I'd been looking to be scorched by a girl that way again. Needless to say, the actual encounters of my so-called real life were nowhere near as enticing as the memory of little Arlene of the baby blues, who, when I last chanced to inspect my 6th grade class portrait, proved to be shockingly bucktoothed, pudgy and cross-eyed."

"Jo-ann" didn't make the top ten. The Playmates are much more noted for their 1959 ditty "Beep Beep." Yet historically they are one of hundreds of replaceable parts in the unseen Top 40 machinery, not as funky or streetwise as the Crests, but never as pretentious as Jay & the Americans. Stretching it, you could call them a latter-year Diamonds, several hits removed. But you wouldn't know it if your only barometer was my fanaticism. By the time I was fourteen I had collected every one of their eight chart singles, including stiffs like "Let's Be Lovers" and "Little Miss Stuckup," plus the immortal "Darling It's Wonderful"/"Island Girl"—their first release, which didn't even make the charts. Encountered at thrift shop, five and ten, Goodwill, and Salvation Army discount center (where I also bought my fall and spring wardrobes), among stacks of other forgotten slices of rock 'n' roll history, fifteen cents apiece, seven for a dollar, these records would evoke such shrieks of ecstasy and recognition on my part that many times I had to be forcibly quelled before being led from the premises, clutching my precious booty. By the time I was sixteen I had *sold* every one of those singles, including "Jo-ann," in an inexplicable fit of capitalistic fervor. Jo-ann, too, I had lost track of, after learning sometime during high school that she'd moved from the city to the dreaded *suburbs*. But somehow her namesake in song trailed me through the years, the melody lodged in the back of my mind, reminder of a youth misspent.

A friend had summoned me to her home soon after the death of her younger brother, ostensibly to appraise the late brother's massive wax estate, his pride and joy. It was a task at which I proved signally maladept. But on the point of leaving, I spotted in the midst of his hundreds and hundreds of vintage albums, in there with *The Paragons Meet the Jesters* and the complete works of Leslie Gore, an LP called *At Play with the Playmates*, with my very own Playmates pictured on the front cover! So that's who they were: these three almost middle-aged, goofy-looking guys, hunched together on a motor scooter—Donny, Morey, and Chic. Immediately I felt my taste in rock 'n' roll, indeed the veracity of my adolescent experience, being cast into doubt. On the other hand, I hadn't heard "Jo-ann" in a good ten years.

"Is it valuable?" my friend inquired when she noticed my sagging jaw, my watery eyes.

"No, not at all," I said, recovering swiftly. "It's worthless. As a matter of fact, it's less than worthless."

"Then why are you drooling?"

"Sinuses," I replied, once again preparing to leave. "I guess I'll just put it back with the others." I was hoping she would offer it to me, but how could she have known that this heavy reader, playgoer, habitué of the experimental films at the downtown *cinématheque*, was also a slavering Playmates fiend, still regretting the cool moves of his teens, made and unmade.

"Sure," she said blithely, "We're going to donate them all to some college record library."

College record library!

"Why don't I just take it with me?" I suggested with a horrid casualness. "Yes, I think I'll just do that. No, don't wrap it," I said, sneaking it under my coat. "We'll call it my fee."

Of course "Jo-ann," when I finally found the time, nerve, appropriate setting, and suitably reverent frame of mind to play it again, proved to be shockingly bucktoothed, pudgy, and cross-eyed.

Morey Carr (real name Cohen) no longer rides a scooter. The Playmate bringing up the rear, he greets me in a white shirt and tie, business suit, when I come to call at his real estate office in New Jersey, just over the George Washington Bridge. I am still in the clawhold of an obsessive dilemma, wondering: Rock 'n' roll? House, kids, pushing fifty? "Miriam, hold my calls," Morey Cohen tells his secretary, as he takes his seat behind the imposing desk. On the other hand, Buddy Holly was no Steve Reeves either.

Seems Morey met Donny and Chic in college in Connecticut, where they played together in dance bands, influenced and inspired by people like Harry James and Les Brown. In 1952 they went on the road as an instrumental and comedy act, billing themselves the Nitwits. In 1956 they came to New York and appeared at the door of Roulette Records on Tenth Avenue in matching shirts, purporting to be a calypso group. Out of this charade came *Calypso with the Playmates*, an album which had also escaped my eagle-eyed youth.

"We had *five* albums," Morey then reveals to my utter as tonishment. "We did one very classy album with all good show tunes. We used a big thirty-six-piece orchestra with Doc Severinsen playing lead trumpet." Another bit of disquieting news: show tunes. Put it together with calypso, lounge comedy, big-band background, and the picture isn't pretty. Wherefore art thou rock 'n' roll?

"At that time rock 'n' roll was not the same rock that we're familiar with today," Morey explains. "It was more or less softer rock. We used to do 'Sh-boom,' which was very popular at the time." Brushing aside the meaner implications of the 'cover' syndrome, I forge on to learn that the Playmates did, at least, participate in an Irvin Feld tour—thirty one-nighters in thirty days, along with the likes of Sam Cooke, Jackie Wilson, LaVern Baker, and Frankie Avalon. "At that time, I have to admit it, we were around twenty-five or twenty-six. Frankie Avalon was sixteen or seventeen years old. They used to carry him out in a cage. The girls wanted to rip his clothes off. I was one of the guys who used to help carry the cage. They didn't want my autograph. They didn't know who I was." Their certified biggie was "Beep Beep," which they recorded in fifteen minutes at the end of a session. "It was written about a year before that, and we'd introduced it at a deejay convention in Kansas City. The deejays loved it. We used to do it with choreography. Donny would put on a pair of sneakers and run around the audience with a horn."

Once they appeared on a "Dick Clark Show" dressed as doctors, lip-synching a turkey called "The Thingamajig." Although I didn't catch that particular performance (didn't even know the record existed), the picture is becoming all too clear. Their downfall came when they had "Wimowey" out and the Tokens covered it with "The Lion Sleeps Tonight," which went to Number 1, while the Playmates' effort fizzled. "We didn't have the falsetto voices; none of us could do a falsetto," Morey recalls. "We could have hired somebody to do it, but we didn't."

So what do rock 'n' roll credentials have to do with anything? The way I see it, the only relevant truth here is that the Playmates gave me "Jo-ann" during my twelfth year when I was deep in sorrow over the unattainable Jo-ann. And no one can remove from the annals of my childhood that searing, sobbing alto sax solo, the soundtrack of my unrequited quest. "Oh yeah," Cohen chuckles, "I remember the guy, Weintraub or something. Every so often I bump into him down at Local 802 and he tells me he was playing out of tune on that record and he was ashamed of it. So I tell him that's all right, we sold about a quarter of a million records."

When was rock 'n' roll supposed to be in tune? I rage inwardly, slumping further in my seat. "For a while there was a battle on between our record and the original," says Morey, his held calls pulsing on his telephone like mysterious signals in some futuristic life-support system. "What were their names? Oh yes, the Twintones. We did a cover on their tune and our version took off. Never heard of the Twintones after that."

Chic is now a schoolteacher and Donny a manufacturer's rep. Morey tried to keep the Playmates going a while longer, but he finally gave it up for real estate. "I still play weddings on weekends," he says. "Once in a while somebody asks me to sing a couple of the old songs."

Leaving suburban Jersey I think about the fate of rock 'n' roll. Aside from the few who went out in billowing headlines, most of the originals sank silently into the middle class, suspended between the Las Vegas lounges of their dreams and the high school hops of their reality. But what about the Twintones? The Twintones, I belatedly realize, were my story all along! Here are these two guys, John and Jim Cunningham, from Hicksville, Long Island, who gave me "Jo-ann," one burst of passion and universal meaning, and that was *it*. Here are these twins, walk-ons in the Top 40, extras, no union cards to fall back on, just one pinch-hit bunt single in the world series and then back to the minors, the car wash, oblivion.

As the car rolls on, I instinctively reach for the AM radio. A hit of the day, some obscure ditty, fills the car for about three minutes, then disappears, leaving me only with the humming in my skull. This humming, which turns to a roar, as the search goes on.

THE PLAYMATES
TOP 40 CHART SINGLES

1958 "Jo-ann"
1958 "Don't Go Home"
1958 "Beep Beep"
1959 "What Is Love"
1960 "Wait for Me"

At Play with the Playmates: Donny, Morey, and Chic.

Appendix

TOP 40 HONOR ROLL

*T*he following lists of the Top 40 singles for 1955–1963 were compiled from a variety of sources that differed on exact placement more often than they agreed. An average was struck, partly by mathematics, partly by personal bias. In whatever combination of sales, radio airplay, and chart longevity, these are as close as any other listing to an accurate honor roll of the most popular songs of these years. Due to certain industry practices—especially in the earlier years when there were still deep racial divisions in chart tabulation—a truly accurate listing is probably an unrealizable ideal.

1955

1. Rock Around the Clock — Bill Haley & His Comets
2. Cherry Pink and Apple Blossom White — Perez Prado
3. The Yellow Rose of Texas — Mitch Miller
4. The Ballad of Davy Crockett — Bill Hayes
5. Sincerely — The McGuire Sisters
6. Ain't That a Shame — Pat Boone
7. Unchained Melody — Les Baxter
8. Sixteen Tons — Tennessee Ernie Ford
9. Hearts of Stone — The Fontane Sisters

10.	Love Is a Many-Splendored Thing	The Four Aces
11.	Unchained Melody	Al Hibbler
12.	Autumn Leaves	Roger Williams
13.	Learnin' the Blues	Frank Sinatra
14.	Let Me Go Lover	Joan Weber
15.	Melody of Love	Billy Vaughn
16.	The Crazy Otto	Johnny Maddox
17.	Tweedle Dee	Georgia Gibbs
18.	Ko Ko Mo	Perry Como
19.	A Blossom Fell	Nat King Cole
20.	Dance with Me, Henry	Georgia Gibbs
21.	Moments to Remember	The Four Lads
22.	Only You	The Platters
23.	I Hear You Knocking	Gale Storm
24.	Earth Angel	The Crew-cuts
25.	Mr. Sandman	The Chordettes
26.	Maybellene	Chuck Berry
27.	Ballad of Davy Crockett	Fess Parker
28.	Ballad of Davy Crockett	Tennessee Ernie Ford
29.	Honey-Babe	Art Mooney
30.	Seventeen	The Fontane Sisters
31.	The Shifting, Whispering Sands	Rusty Draper
32.	Something's Gotta Give	The McGuire Sisters
33.	Seventeen	Boyd Bennett & His Rockets
34.	The Shifting, Whispering Sands	Billy Vaughn
35.	How Important Can It Be	Joni James
36.	The Yellow Rose of Texas	Johnny Desmond
37.	Melody of Love	The Four Aces
38.	He	Al Hibbler
39.	Hard to Get	Gisele MacKenzie
40.	Tina Marie	Perry Como

1956

1.	Don't Be Cruel	Elvis Presley
2.	Heartbreak Hotel	Elvis Presley
3.	The Wayward Wind	Gogi Grant

4.	My Prayer	The Platters
5.	Lisbon Antigua	Nelson Riddle
6.	Memories Are Made of This	Dean Martin
7.	Moonglow and Theme from "Picnic"	Morris Stoloff
8.	Hound Dog	Elvis Presley
9.	Rock and Roll Waltz	Kay Starr
10.	The Poor People of Paris	Les Baxter
11.	The Great Pretender	The Platters
12.	Whatever Will Be Will Be	Doris Day
13.	I Want You, I Need You, I Love You	Elvis Presley
14.	Blue Suede Shoes	Carl Perkins
15.	Honky Tonk	Bill Doggett
16.	Love Me Tender	Elvis Presley
17.	Canadian Sunset	Hugo Winterhalter and Eddie Heywood
18.	Hot Diggity	Perry Como
19.	I Almost Lost My Mind	Pat Boone
20.	The Green Door	Jim Lowe
21.	No, Not Much	The Four Lads
22.	Just Walking in the Rain	Johnnie Ray
23.	I'm in Love Again	Fats Domino
24.	Allegheny Moon	Patti Page
25.	Sixteen Tons	Tennessee Ernie Ford
26.	Tonight You Belong to Me	Patience & Prudence
27.	Ivory Tower	Cathy Carr
28.	Why Do Fools Fall in Love	Frankie Lymon & the Teenagers
29.	Singing the Blues	Guy Mitchell
30.	Standing on the Corner	The Four Lads
31.	The Flying Saucer	Buchanan & Goodman
32.	On the Street Where You Live	Vic Damone
33.	Blueberry Hill	Fats Domino
34.	The Magic Touch	The Platters
35.	See You Later, Alligator	Bill Haley & His Comets
36.	True Love	Bing Crosby & Grace Kelly
37.	Band of Gold	Don Cherry
38.	I'll Be Home	Pat Boone
39.	Be-Bop-a-Lula	Gene Vincent & His Blue Caps
40.	Born to Be with You	The Chordettes

1957

1.	All Shook Up	Elvis Presley
2.	Love Letters in the Sand	Pat Boone
3.	Young Love	Tab Hunter
4.	Tammy	Debbie Reynolds
5.	Young Love	Sonny James
6.	Little Darlin'	The Diamonds
7.	Round and Round	Perry Como
8.	Let Me Be Your Teddy Bear	Elvis Presley
9.	So Rare	Jimmy Dorsey
10.	Don't Forbid Me	Pat Boone
11.	Bye Bye Love	Everly Brothers
12.	Honeycomb	Jimmy Rodgers
13.	Jailhouse Rock	Elvis Presley
14.	Butterfly	Charlie Gracie
15.	Wake Up Little Suzie	Everly Brothers
16.	Party Doll	Buddy Knox
17.	Diana	Paul Anka
18.	Too Much	Elvis Presley
19.	Chances Are	Johnny Mathis
20.	You Send Me	Sam Cooke
21.	Singing the Blues	Guy Mitchell
22.	A Teenager's Romance	Ricky Nelson
23.	Butterfly	Andy Williams
24.	A White Sport Coat	Marty Robbins
25.	Come Go with Me	The Dell Vikings
26.	Raunchy	Bill Justis
27.	Day-o	Harry Belafonte
28.	That'll Be the Day	The Crickets
29.	Marianne	The Hilltoppers
30.	It's Not for Me to Say	Johnny Mathis
31.	Gone	Ferlin Husky
32.	I'm Gonna Sit Right Down and Write Myself a Letter	Billy Williams
33.	School Day	Chuck Berry
34.	Silhouettes	The Rays
35.	Dark Moon	Gale Storm

36. Searching   The Coasters
37. Whole Lot of Shakin' Going On   Jerry Lee Lewis
38. Banana Boat Song   The Tarriers
39. Old Cape Cod   Patti Page
40. Be-Bop Baby   Ricky Nelson

1958

1. Nel Blu Dipinto Di Blu (Volare)   Domenico Modungo
2. All I Have to Do Is Dream   Everly Brothers
3. It's All in the Game   Tommy Edwards
4. Witch Doctor   David Seville
5. Tequila   The Champs
6. Patricia   Perez Prado
7. Don't   Elvis Presley
8. At the Hop   Danny & the Juniors
9. The Purple People Eater   Sheb Wooley
10. Little Star   The Elegants
11. Catch a Falling Star   Perry Como
12. He's Got the Whole World (in His
    Hands)   Laurie London
13. Get a Job   The Silhouettes
14. Twilight Time   The Platters
15. Bird Dog   The Everly Brothers
16. Return to Me   Dean Martin
17. It's Only Make Believe   Conway Twitty
18. Poor Little Fool   Ricky Nelson
19. Yakety Yak   The Coasters
20. Sail Along Silvery Moon   Billy Vaughn
21. Rock-in Robin   Bobby Day
22. Secretly   Jimmy Rodgers
23. Tom Dooley   The Kingston Trio
24. Wear My Ring Around Your Neck   Elvis Presley
25. Sugartime   The McGuire Sisters
26. To Know Him Is to Love Him   The Teddy Bears
27. Topsy II   Cozy Cole
28. Stood Up   Ricky Nelson

29.	Sweet Little Sixteen	Chuck Berry
30.	Splish Splash	Bobby Darin
31.	Lollipop	The Chordettes
32.	Just a Dream	Jimmy Clanton
33.	Who's Sorry Now	Connie Francis
34.	Tears on My Pillow	Little Anthony & the Imperials
35.	The Stroll	The Diamonds
36.	Hard Headed Woman	Elvis Presley
37.	The Chipmunk Song	The Chipmunks / David Seville
38.	Tea for Two Cha-Cha	Tommy Dorsey Orch / Warren Covington
39.	April Love	Pat Boone
40.	When	The Kalin Twins

1959

1.	Mack the Knife	Bobby Darin
2.	The Battle of New Orleans	Johnny Horton
3.	Venus	Frankie Avalon
4.	The Three Bells	The Browns
5.	Come Softly to Me	The Fleetwoods
6.	Lonely Boy	Paul Anka
7.	Stagger Lee	Lloyd Price
8.	Personality	Lloyd Price
9.	Sleep Walk	Santo & Johnny
10.	Smoke Gets in Your Eyes	The Platters
11.	Mr. Blue	The Fleetwoods
12.	Put Your Head on My Shoulder	Paul Anka
13.	Kansas City	Wilbert Harrison
14.	Dream Lover	Bobby Darin
15.	Charlie Brown	The Coasters
16.	The Happy Organ	Dave "Baby" Cortez
17.	Pink Shoelaces	Dodie Stevens
18.	Quiet Village	Martin Denny
19.	Donna	Richie Valens
20.	Sorry (I Ran All the Way Home)	The Impalas

21. Sea of Love   Phil Phillips
22. There Goes My Baby   The Drifters
23. A Big Hunk o' Love   Elvis Presley
24. ('Til) I Kissed You   Everly Brothers
25. Lipstick on Your Collar   Connie Francis
26. A Fool Such As I   Elvis Presley
27. Sixteen Candles   The Crests
28. My Heart Is an Open Book   Carl Dobkins, Jr.
29. Don't You Know   Della Reese
30. A Teenager in Love   Dion & the Belmonts
31. Lavender Blue   Sammy Turner
32. Tiger   Fabian
33. I'm Gonna Get Married   Lloyd Price
34. It's Just a Matter of Time   Brook Benton
35. Waterloo   Stonewall Jackson
36. Teen Beat   Sandy Nelson
37. Heartaches by the Number   Guy Mitchell
38. Kookie, Kookie (Lend Me Your Comb)   Edd Byrnes & Connie Stevens
39. My Happiness   Connie Francis
40. Red River Rock   Johnny & the Hurricanes

1960

1. Theme from "A Summer Place"   Percy Faith
2. Running Bear   Johnny Preston
3. Cathy's Clown   The Everly Brothers
4. Stuck on You   Elvis Presley
5. It's Now or Never   Elvis Presley
6. Teen Angel   Mark Dinning
7. I'm Sorry   Brenda Lee
8. El Paso   Marty Robbins
9. Everybody's Somebody's Fool   Connie Francis
10. The Twist   Chubby Checker
11. He'll Have to Go   Jim Reeves
12. Itsy Bitsy Teenie Weenie Yellow Polka
    Dot Bikini   Brian Hyland

13.	Save the Last Dance for Me	The Drifters
14.	Handy Man	Jimmy Jones
15.	Greenfields	The Brothers Four
16.	Wild One	Bobby Rydell
17.	My Heart Has a Mind of Its Own	Connie Francis
18.	Alley Oop	The Hollywood Argyles
19.	Why	Frankie Avalon
20.	Walk—Don't Run	The Ventures
21.	Chain Gang	Sam Cooke
22.	Only the Lonely	Roy Orbison
23.	Good Timin'	Jimmy Jones
24.	Are You Lonesome Tonight	Elvis Presley
25.	Mr. Custer	Larry Verne
26.	Puppy Love	Paul Anka
27.	I Want to Be Wanted	Brenda Lee
28.	Sweet Nothin's	Brenda Lee
29.	Stay	Maurice Williams & the Zodiacs
30.	Burning Bridges	Jack Scott
31.	Night	Jackie Wilson
32.	Georgia on My Mind	Ray Charles
33.	The Big Hurt	Timi Yuro
34.	What in the World's Come Over You	Jack Scott
35.	Because They're Young	Duane Eddy
36.	Sixteen Reasons	Connie Stevens
37.	Finger Poppin' Time	Hank Ballard & the Midnighters
38.	Where or When	Dion & the Belmonts
39.	Baby (You've Got What It Takes)	Dinah Washington & Brook Benton
40.	Way Down Yonder in New Orleans	Freddy Cannon

1961

1.	Tossin' and Turnin'	Bobby Lewis
2.	Michael	The Highwaymen

3.	Calcutta	Lawrence Welk
4.	Pony Time	Chubby Checker
5.	Will You Love Me Tomorrow	The Shirelles
6.	Runaway	Del Shannon
7.	Take Good Care of My Baby	Bobby Vee
8.	Exodus	Ferrante & Teicher
9.	Crying	Roy Orbison
10.	Running Scared	Roy Orbison
11.	Wooden Heart	Joe Dowell
12.	Travelin' Man	Ricky Nelson
13.	Raindrops	Dee Clark
14.	Wheels	The String-a-longs
15.	The Boll Weevil Song	Brook Benton
16.	Mother-in-Law	Ernie K-Doe
17.	A Quarter to Three	Gary U.S. Bonds
18.	Last Night	The Mar-kays
19.	My True Story	The Jive Five
20.	Blue Moon	The Marcels
21.	Hit the Road Jack	Ray Charles
22.	Dedicated to the One I Love	The Shirelles
23.	Shop Around	The Miracles
24.	A Hundred Pounds of Clay	Gene McDaniels
25.	Wonderland by Night	Bert Kaempfert
26.	Where the Boys Are	Connie Francis
27.	The Mountain's High	Dick & Deedee
28.	The Bristol Stomp	The Dovells
29.	On the Rebound	Floyd Cramer
30.	Apache	Jorgen Ingmann
31.	I Like It Like That	Chris Kenner
32.	Don't Worry	Marty Robbins
33.	Sad Movies	Sue Thompson
34.	Surrender	Elvis Presley
35.	Calendar Girl	Neil Sedaka
36.	Runaround Sue	Dion
37.	Big Bad John	Jimmy Dean
38.	Moody River	Pat Boone
39.	The Lion Sleeps Tonight	The Tokens
40.	Daddy's Home	Shep & the Limelights

1962

1. Johnny Angel — Shelley Fabares
2. I Can't Stop Loving You — Ray Charles
3. Peppermint Twist — Joey Dee & the Starlighters
4. Stranger on the Shore — Acker Bilk
5. Soldier Boy — The Shirelles
6. Mashed Potato Time — Dee Dee Sharp
7. Roses Are Red — Bobby Vinton
8. Hey Baby — Bruce Channel
9. The Stripper — David Rose
10. Duke of Earl — Gene Chandler
11. Loco-motion — Little Eva
12. Breaking Up Is Hard to Do — Neil Sedaka
13. The Twist — Chubby Checker
14. Ramblin' Rose — Nat Cole
15. Sherry — The Four Seasons
16. Big Girls Don't Cry — The Four Seasons
17. The Wanderer — Dion
18. Telstar — The Tornadoes
19. Let Me In — The Sensations
20. Sheila — Tommy Roe
21. Midnight in Moscow — Kenny Ball
22. Palisades Park — Freddy Cannon
23. The Wah Watusi — The Orlons
24. Monster Mash — Bobby Pickett & the Crypt Kickers

25. Good Luck Charm — Elvis Presley
26. He's a Rebel — The Crystals
27. Norman — Sue Thompson
28. Sealed with a Kiss — Brian Hyland
29. Slow Twistin' — Chubby Checker
30. Don't Break the Heart That Loves You — Connie Francis
31. Love Letters — Ketty Lester
32. The One Who Really Loves You — Mary Wells
33. She Cried — Jay & the Americans
34. Party Lights — Claudine Clark
35. It Keeps Right on a-Hurting — Johnny Tillotson

36.	Green Onions	Booker T & the MGs
37.	Return to Sender	Elvis Presley
38.	Crying in the Rain	Everly Brothers
39.	Playboy	The Marvelettes
40.	What's Your Name	Don & Juan

1963

1.	Fingertips, Part Two	Little Stevie Wonder
2.	He's So Fine	The Chiffons
3.	Blue Velvet	Bobby Vinton
4.	My Boyfriend's Back	The Angels
5.	Hey Paula	Paul & Paula
6.	I Will Follow Him	Little Peggy March
7.	Louie, Louie	The Kingsmen
8.	Can't Get Used to Losing You	Andy Williams
9.	The End of the World	Skeeter Davis
10.	Sukiyaki	Kyo Sakimoto
11.	Surfin' U.S.A.	The Beach Boys
12.	Walk Like a Man	The Four Seasons
13.	So Much in Love	The Tymes
14.	Rhythm of the Rain	The Cascades
15.	Walk Right In	The Rooftop Singers
16.	Sugar Shack	Jimmy Gilmer & the Fireballs
17.	Our Day Will Come	Ruby & the Romantics
18.	If You Wanna Be Happy	Jimmy Soul
19.	It's My Party	Leslie Gore
20.	Easier Said Than Done	The Essex
21.	Puff (The Magic Dragon)	Peter, Paul & Mary
22.	Surf City	Jan & Dean
23.	Limbo Rock	Chubby Checker
24.	I Love You Because	Al Martino
25.	Go Away Little Girl	Steve Lawrence
26.	Hello Stranger	Barbara Lewis
27.	Blowin' in the Wind	Peter, Paul & Mary

28. You're the Reason I'm Living — Bobby Darin
29. Ruby Baby — Dion
30. You Can't Sit Down — The Dovells
31. Pipeline — The Chantays
32. I'm Leaving It Up to You — Dale & Grace
33. Up on the Roof — The Drifters
34. Wipeout — The Safaris
35. Be My Baby — The Ronettes
36. Dominique — The Singing Nun
37. Deep Purple — April Stevens & Nino Tempo
38. Candy Girl — The Four Seasons
39. Hello Muddah, Hello Fadduh — Allan Sherman
40. If I Had a Hammer — Trini Lopez

Index